PPL IN A DEPOT

PPL IN A DEPOT

Gary Sullivan

ROOF BOOKS
NEW YORK

ISBN: 978-1-931824-28-6
Library of Congress Catalog Card Number: 2008921462

Some of this work was published, in slightly different form, in the following: *Arras*; *canwehaveourballback?*; *E-X-C-H-A-N-G-E-V-A-L-U-E-S: The Second XV Interviews*; *Jacket*; *Ocho*; *Pom2*; and *Shampoo*. My thanks to the editors of these anthologies, journals and webzines.

State of the Arts
NYSCA

This book was made possible, in part, with public funds from the New York State Council on the Arts, a state agency.

Roof Books are distributed by
Small Press Distribution
1341 Seventh Street
Berkeley, CA. 94710-1403
Phone orders: 800-869-7553
www.spdbooks.org

Roof Books are published by
Segue Foundation
300 Bowery
New York, NY 10012
seguefoundation.com

Contents

I REALLY SO DETEST ANY "OCCUPATION"! GIVEN EACH DAY THE CHOICE: WORK, OR ONE HARD PUNCH TO THE FACE, I WOULD PREFER TO BE PUNCHED!
TELL ME, SALIERI: WOULD YOU DRINK A GLASS OF MILK CONTAINING 1,000 PUS CELLS?
WHY, HEAVENS, NO!!!
THE AVERAGE 12-OUNCE GLASS OF MILK IN AMERICA CONTAINS
112,899,408 PUS CELLS!

MOZART & SALIERI

MOZART & SALIERI

Premiered at the Line Reading Series at the Drawing Center, New York City, December 3, 2002. Directed by Gary Sullivan, with the following cast:

MOZART	Brian Kim Stefans
SALIERI	Gary Sullivan
FAN	Susan Landers

Other performances:

La Tazza, Philadelphia, December 13, 2003. Directed by Gary Sullivan and starring C.A. Conrad (MOZART), Gary Sullivan (SALIERI), and Nada Gordon (FAN).

Stephanie Young's House Party reading series, Oakland, California, December 2004. Directed by Gary Sullivan and starring Rodney Koeneke (MOZART), Gary Sullivan (SALIERI), and Nada Gordon (FAN).

The Medicine Show Theater, New York City, June 14–30, 2007. Directed by Barbara Vann and starring Mark J. Dempsey (MOZART), Vince Phillip (SALIERI), and Chorus (FAN).

Scene One: *Starbucks.*

SALIERI: You can't get a decent cup of coffee in NYC
But it's not like Heaven is awash in mochaccino
Nor as plain as I-IV-V. God, I love
"The Arts"! Even as a child, in our ancient church
The organ would send forth its froth
More horrible than the whole Toledo Symphony!
I was lost in it—such sweet frosting. I turned
From idle pastimes early: Terrified of bugs, of
Smarmy talking animals; karaoke drove me into fits
Of madness and rage. I developed my own method
Of tying bows in shoelaces, based loosely
On a set of blueprints for the Bell Folding Organ.
From E. Power Biggs to Richard "Groove" Holmes
I spent every waking moment spinning sides
Till my mind was like a station wagon filled
With popcorn: "Diagonal percussion trophic resiny
Propane pomegranate adulterate Creole integrand
Americanism rodent commandeer," etc.! I composed
In secret; didn't dare yet dream of glory.
Sleepless, I stopped eating beef—soon, other
"Wild game" followed. Tasting of raptures & tears
Of inspiration, I'd burn my work, not calories.
My thoughts rose in flames only to vanish
In little tufts of foam. When "El Lobster Rojo"—
The Great Gluck himself!—appeared, unfolding new
Mysteries, did I not give up all I'd known before?
Did I not briskly follow him, murmurless
Into the infinities of art's lofty levels?
What living louse out there claims proud Salieri
Was ever that trampled snake, an envious man
Only quick to bite gravel & dust in impotence?
Nobody! ... Now, though—I myself must say it—
Now, I'm floating in the green liquid of
The Jealous Sea. Adrift, cut off from the world—
O Heaven, where is thy justice, when the holy gift
Immortal genius comes not as reward
For life's flat surfaces covered with piles
Of sweet frosting—but lights its radiance instead

In heads of folly and frivolity? Oh, Mozart, Mozart!

[MOZART *enters.*]

MOZART: Aha! You saw me! (Or must've heard the flapping
Of the pet door.) Knock, knock!

SALIERI: Urgh—you've been standing there this whole time?

MOZART: I would have gotten here sooner, but I had
Cloud strife. Just kidding: I was trying to find
NSYNC—I want to sit in with them tonight.
Oh, Salieri, my friend, you wouldn't believe
How many people recognized me and how many autographs
I've had to sign. I had no choice but to bring
Stragglers here!

FAN [*Tearing off T-shirt*]: Oh my god, I'm such a fan, will you
Sign my midriff?

[*Laughing salaciously,* MOZART *signs.* FAN *leaves,*
awash in giggles. MOZART *chuckles.*]

SALIERI: And you can laugh at that?

MOZART: Oh come, Salieri, don't you think it's funny?

SALIERI: Would Alighieri debrief Yoko's loofa?

MOZART: As a conversationalist, you've come unfastened.
I'll come again some other time.

[MOZART *wags a huge notebook in* SALIERI*'s face.*]

SALIERI: Wait,
What's that?

MOZART: A mere trifle. Last night at a
Wedding, I had a few too many. There may
Have been some unsightly gyrating on the floor

A spilled cocktail here and there, a profane
Remark made w/in earshot of the grandmother.
I got a ride home with an elderly, religious, non-
Drinking uncle. When I woke bright and early this
Morning, my head was throbbing—just throbbing
With new ideas! I jotted them down. I wanted
Your opinion, but you're in a mood.

SALIERI: Oh, Mozart, Mozart, wedding mishaps are not
Forgotten, but become lore! Sit down.
I'm listening.

MOZART [*Opening the notebook*]: "Son thinker's recollection
Methought tatter marketplaces sullying
Vasectomy hygiene lore's SOS weaves cardiacs
Sot wolverine's authoritarianism breathlessness's
Fractals topsoils disabled Iowa's Va's
Restrictively austerest VAT irreproachable
Loading's deity's misconducting disables
Aridity's overqualified Tod spy refurbishing
Lothario inveigles soapiest ambitions
Cantonese shoddiness hogsheads pungent procurement
Congratulating confounding cowhide gunslinger
Supplement's pulpits henpecks galvanometers
Companied terms Rx's architectural SST Gujranwala
Cushions leotard's reformatory's sierras
Genres obeys bloodsheds St.'s approval clanged."

SALIERI: You were bringing this to me, and yet could stop
To sign some fan's midriff? God, Mozart,
You are unworthy of yourself.

MOZART: You like?

SALIERI: What profundity! What boldness!
What perfect foam!

MOZART: Oh, come now, Salieri.
What's foam to the starving man?

SALIERI: Dinner is on me: Red Lobster!

MOZART: Gladly.
But let me first address
Why we exist.

[MOZART *exits.*]

SALIERI: He looked fine when he came in,
Although he did complain of a headache.
I've got to stop him! He'd want me to, yes
Even if it means killing him. Yes ... the baby eats
First pablum, then solid food ... to snivel or
Grovel about it would be monumentally—
Aaaah-CHOO! Oh, insult! He uplifts even the wingless
Dust & I can no longer resist fate.

[SALIERI *pulls a bright red frog from his pocket.*]

The word "amphibian" comes from the Greek meaning
"Double-life." This group includes
Poison dart frogs: Isora's final gift.
For eighteen years I've carried it with me.
Tonight, the "adult door prize drawing" will be held
As usual!

[*Curtain. End of* SCENE ONE.]

Scene Two: *Red Lobster.*

SALIERI: What's wrong? You seem adrift on some other sea ...

MOZART [*Bombed off his ass.*]: Wolfgang Amadeus smashed another spent cigarette
His third in the past hour, into the over-
Flowing ashtray on the Formica table. Grey curlicues
Of smoke from this last contribution hung
In the air, unnoticed. [*To* SALIERI:] I know why
You're here with me right now. To balance
The goodness. [*Covers mouth with hand.*] Wolfgang
Was being a *bitch*! [*Suddenly very serious, sober.*]
I had this horrible nightmare last night. I was peeking
Into this Chinese-looking room
From outside. I felt scared, saw aunts & uncles
Hanging from a pole upside down. Auntie
Looked sadly back at me. I walked around the building
& saw this big sort of old guy—Mexican?—like
Dino from Fear Factory. He had a beard, a blue shirt
Or pants. He was standing in front of, blocking
The sun. I started screaming.

SALIERI: "Stars twinkle in glory, the moon gives her light
Still I weep for the sun
But not from childish fright ..." Where love is
Concerned, too much is like Beaumarchais, who
In his feathery "wah-wah," oft remarked:
"Salieri, old friend, when thoughts come ...
Uncork the language!"

MOZART: Vonnegut's volumetric voluble
Voltaire's volstead volcanic vol voegelin vocalists
Verdi's verbatim vera venomous venom—
You and Beaumarchais were pals, weren't you?
Yes, it was for him you wrote a lovely
Work, later co-opted by a car company. Is it true
Beaumarchais once poisoned somebody?

SALIERI: No,
He avoided everything.

MOZART: Besides, he was a genius
Like me. And genius and villainy
Are incompatible, aren't they?

SALIERI [*Pulls out his frog*]: When I was young, I refused to try frog legs—
By my count, every day 40,000 children starve!
To feed one meat-eater for a year requires
Three and a half acres; it takes
One half acre for a lacto-ovo vegetarian
One sixth acre for a vegan. Animal waste
Accounts for more than ten times the
Water pollution caused by human hand
The meat industry dumps three times as much
Harmful waste in the waters as the nation's
Industries combined. Oh, Mozart, Mozart!
Too late I learned frog legs to be a delicacy!

MOZART [*Taking the frog; considering.*]: On a typical dairy farm, cows stand on concrete
Chained by the neck in huge sheds, are milked
By machines. To boost production, some farmers
Inject cows with synthetic growth hormones
Which increase the cows' risk of developing mastitis
A painful condition that will cause one's udders
To become so heavy they drag on the ground.
Tell me, Salieri: Would you drink a glass of milk
Containing 1,000 pus cells?

SALIERI: Why, heavens, no!

MOZART: The average 12-ounce glass of milk in America
Contains 112,899,408 pus cells!

[MOZART *swallows the frog whole, then raises his glass.*]

MOZART: To health,
My friend, and to Mozart and Salieri, joined
At the harmony. [*Throws his napkin down.*]
Enough. I'm sated.

[MOZART *hoists backpack to table, pulls out his massive notebook. Opens, thumbs through.*]

MOZART: Salieri, listen: My Requiem:
[*Begins writing in his notebook, reading*
aloud as he goes.] "Quote I am only a bundle of
Masks & you can't fight a duel with that unquote.
Quote Exotic carnivores in zoos are fed cattle
Carcasses & there have been a number of reports
Of TSE cases since 1990 including puma,
Cheetah, ocelot, tiger and lion unquote."
Ohhh. [*Takes a sip of wine to steady himself.*]
"Quote My ocelot ate my tax forms, submitted by
Anonymous unquote. Quote Being fat is as pre-
Determined as death em-dash bitches ain't shit
Unquote. Quote If time/talent/money were no object
What would your dream occupation be question mark
Unquote." [*Looks up at* SALIERI.] You're weeping?

SALIERI: These tears—I really so detest any "occupation"!
Given each day the choice: work, or one hard punch
To the face, I would prefer to be punched.
Within a year, my face would be unrecognizable
But think of how I would have spent my days!
Mozart, dear friend, these tears ...
Less than nothing. Play on, your Requiem—
Saturate my soul with foam!

MOZART: Can you imagine
Salieri, if everyone stopped working
Stayed home & counterfeited art? Why
We'd all starve to death! The likes of us,
We chosen ones are few, happily idle
Not a care for mere usefulness. [*A sudden spasm.*]
But this blog seems to have untickled me:

I must jet or be made someone's trophy.

SALIERI: Farewell, Mozart. See you soon.

[MOZART *exits.*]

SALIERI: You will be
Offline a long time, my friend. But
What was it you said? Genius and villainy
Are incompatible. Is it true? What about
Damien Hirst? In short time all colors
Intermingle with black & white; art like heat
Of sun on sea, foams for all maddened by thirst!

[*Curtain.*]

THE SEPARATION OF CHURCH AND STATE

THE SEPARATION OF CHURCH AND STATE

THOMAS JEFFERSON
ANGEL
AMERICA
COUNSELOR
JUDGE
TEACHER

THOMAS JEFFERSON *paces back and forth holding a candle and a letter.*]

JEFFERSON [*Reading aloud*]: "Dear Sir,

"Among the millions in America and Europe who rejoice in your election to office, I embrace the first opportunity which I have enjoyed in my singular capacity, since your Inauguration, to express the following:

a) ALL CANADIANS residing in the United States should be shot

b) DOG BREEDERS should be shot

c) People who think I'm an idiot and an (expletive) and unpatriotic—they should be shot.

"And though my mode of expression may be less courtly and pompous than what many others clothe their addresses with, I beg you, Sir to believe, that none are more sincere.

(Signed) Stephen Ephraim Nehemiah Dodgerobbins"

[JEFFERSON *looks at the letter, puts it down. Takes out his quill pen and starts to write at his desk.*]

JEFFERSON [*Reading aloud*]: "Dear Mr. S.E.N. Dodgerobbins,

"The affectionate sentiments of esteem and approbation, which you are so good as to express towards me, give me the highest satisfaction.

"That said, comments on this site are moderated, and I will reject comments containing wackjob conspiracy theories about aspartame, splenda, BVO, etc.

"Further, if you want to criticize, say, my relationships with women, or my personality—strike that—*your perception of* my personality, don't be shocked if—"

[ANGEL *enters*. JEFFERSON *looks up*.]

JEFFERSON [*Startled*]: How did you get in here? I was certain I asked for no interr—

ANGEL [*Sparkle noise*]: I am an Angel on a passionate spiritual journey and I would like to share my message with you, Thomas. It is a unique—

JEFFERSON: "Thomas"? With all due respect, you are conversing with the President of the United States of America.

ANGEL [*Sparkle noise*]: My voice is like whispers of the wind gently blowing through soft wind chimes, yet very clear. Can you feel the coming days of America surround you with electrifying light and energy that covers you whole body?

JEFFERSON: What? Are you referring to what I just posted?

[*Sudden light show,* AMERICA *trickles in, stage left.*]

JEFFERSON: What manner of witchery is this?

SHIRLEY WOOD: Hey Tiffany, have you seen Gina?

RONALD WEINER: She's in the gym hoping the principal puts ornaments on the Christmas tree.

JANE MINICUCCI: Sounds like a swell!

TEDDY TOOTHMAN: People who decorate their house for Christmas should be shot—

VOICE [*Over intercom*]: Good morning, everyone! Please rise.

[AMERICA *stands with hands over hearts and recites.*]

ALL: "I pledge allegiance to the underclass, and fuck all y'all fucking elitist ass monkeys U shd B shot onsite, I will not be caught livin' in a dead end, I'm here to represent, and spit right in the face of the establishment."

JEFFERSON: I see nothing "off topic" here! They are simply paying homage—

ANGEL [*Sparkle noise*]: Yes, Thomas, but we have only begun our journey ...

["*Wild West*" *saloon piano music, up.*]

CHRISTINE FUNKENSTEIN: People who label themselves Hopeless Romantics are stupid and should be shot, hung, disemboweled, and decapitated—

COUNSELOR: I beg your pardon?

MARY HAIR: You heard 'er! People who "can't be bothered" reading subtitles should be shot in the fucking kneecaps and left to bleed!

COUNSELOR: Now see here! [*"Wild West" music stops abruptly.*] I will respect your point of view ma'am, but I don't appreciate your tone!

BONUS MILLER: I don't care what you appreciate! People who chew with their mouths open should be shot. People who lick the ends of their fingers should be forced to lick the ends of OTHER people's fingers, the very fingers used to squeeze—

COUNSELOR: Ma'am you are way over the line! You should be preparing to face problems on Earth, not in some fairyland called Your Opinion!

WILLA MUNCH: Doppler radar? Give me a fucking break: all weather people should be shot—

VINCENT D. NIPPLE: Well, anyone who creates a Web page that blares music at me like that should be shot—

JANG KONGTHONG: People who eat poached eggs need to be tied to an ant mound and covered in something ants like eating and then shot—

COUNSELOR: I believe the majority of Americans AND their parents would disagree with you ma'am.

PATRICIA PURDY: If you don't like it, why don't you sue us?

SUSAN CUDLIPP: I worked at Wendy's for about two years and I personally think that anyone who uses any of the following should be shot:

"Aks" instead of "ask"
"Alrighty then"
"At the end of the day"
"Back in the day"
People who refer to popular vacation spot Cabo San Lucas as "Cabo"
"Ciao," "peace out," or other annoying "hip" ways to say goodbye
"Conversate"
"Don't go there"
"Fantabulous"
"FYI" (like you know something I don't)
"Good to go"
"Have a good one"
"I'd hit that"
"It's all good"
"My bad"
"No biggie"
"No can do"
"Quote Unquote" (with or without accompanying hand gestures)
"So, I was like"
"24/7"
"With all due respect" (something disrespectful comes next!)
"X is the new Y"
"You go girl"

JOAN FLEMSAK: You go girl!

COUNSELOR: With all due respect—

[JEFFERSON *puts his foot down.*]

JEFFERSON: Treason! My eyes behold treason! False images that will never come to pass!

ANGEL [*Sparkle noise*]: But it will happen, Thomas. Your own words, "separation of church and state," will be used against you.

JEFFERSON [*Pacing*]: This vision must never endure. The consequences would be monumental!

[JUDGE *enters.*]

JUDGE: "Judging": Making a final say based on the facts as you perceive them: "People who bring babies in public places should be shot on sight." Everson vs. Board of Education, 1947. [*Gavel sound.*]

"People who giggle at screenings of Brokeback Mountain need to be guided out of the theatre and shot." Engel vs. Vitale, 1962. [*Gavel sound.*]

"People who use masking tape should be shot." Abington vs. Schempp, 1963; "People who pull the last inches of tape down inside the reel don't even deserve the dignity of a firing squad. Reed vs. van Hoven, 1965. [*Gavel sound.*]

"People who sign themselves with some bit of 'wise' twaddle, which usually reads like something one might find in a ghastly Xmas cracker, should be shot." Commissioner of Education vs. School Committee of Leyden, 1971. [*Gavel sound.*]

"People who don't pull over to let an emergency vehicle pass should be shot on site, brought back to life, kicked in the crotch, strangled and allowed to choke back to death on their own sweaty gym socks, and while they are gasping for air you kick them down and allow a 240kg person to sit on their chest while a homeless drunk steals their shoes." Florey vs. Sioux Falls, 1979. [*Gavel sound.*]

"You like Warren Zevon and you don't even listen to him, you should be shot." Stone vs. Gramm, 1980. [*Gavel sound.*]

"There are the people who never got over the fact that 'Seinfeld' ended. These are people who should be shot." Ring vs. Grand Forks Public School District, 1980. [*Gavel sound.*]

"Vegansexuals are people who do not eat any meat or animal products ... it's an unforgivable disdain of your own species for which you should be shot." Lanner vs. Wimmer, 1981. [*Gavel sound.*]

JEFFERSON: Men from our great country made this so? Men from our nation will make these abominations laws?

ANGEL [*Sparkle noise*]: Listen, Thomas ... do you hear that?

[*Pause. Silence.*]

JEFFERSON [*Confused*]: But ... I hear nothing.

ANGEL [*Sparkle noise*]: Exactly, Thomas, absolute silence. So they continue.

JUDGE [*Continues*]: "People who call themselves 'sk8rs' or who use the phrase 'mad player skills' should be shot." Roberts vs. Madigan, 1990. [*Gavel sound.*]

"The Only People Who Should Be Wearing the Crocs are my darling children (not that I'm biased) ... everyone else should be shot." Washegesic vs. Bloomingdale, 1993. [*Gavel sound.*]

JEFFERSON: Be gone with this image! I wish to see it no more!

[ANGEL *raises hand,* JUDGE *exits stage left.*]

ANGEL [*Sparkle noise*]: The America you know, Thomas, is founded upon truth. The America that is coming is not.

[*Blackout.* AMERICA *trickles back in.*]

DONALD FINNERFROCK: Gah! Damn all the flamers to hell!

ROSE DICKERHOOF: No, they might like that due to all the flames there.

TEACHER: Alright guys, cut it out.

KATHLEEN FUGGIT: Flamers are spoiled little brats who don't know what it's like to ACTUALLY be creative. I mean, seriously, they don't appreciate other people's work, which we have worked so hard to create.

TEACHER: I said be quiet!

ROBERT BLEWETT: I like people who give CONTRUCTIVE comments. If they think a character is acting OOC, or if an OC acts like a Mary-sue, I like it when people tell me that, since I want to make my fic even better. If you hate the characters, the plot, the couple, that's your problem, not ours.

TEACHER: SHUT IT, NOW! [*Slams book on stand.*]

WET HUANG: I'm a CYOA writer and I've been getting those kind of flames too. They even threaented to BURN DOWN my HOUSE and kill my li'l bro.

TEACHER: This be my third and last warning to you!

JESSIE JOINT: What the hell's up with U ppl?! I mean CYOA fics are great! Nothing's wrong with 'em! Ppl love'em!!!! I sure do!!!!!!!!

TEACHER: SHUT UP!!! SHUT THE FUCK UP!!!

SONDRA SCHATS: To me, flamers are just stupid little whinny bitches that don't got a life, so just kill the flamers, burn them with their own flames and be happy cause that would make me happy. Flamers suck and they should die.

TEACHER: I hate you I hate you I hate you! I hate each and every one of you!

VERA GAY: I thought Flamers were meant as fags, the last time I checked ... looks like this petition was ill-concived ... morons. Flamers are Fags, which I plan later to contain my thoughts on.

TEACHER [*Spotlight, center stage*]: HIS PLAN?? So was His plan for me to live a life full of pain, to live with love one minute, and for the next to not know any, to watch my brother live in pain and grief, just because Scott Smith felt like driving drunk that night?

NECKLALL KHOOBLALL [*From the shadows*]: *currently too busy trying to rid the world of flamers to respond* Bwahaha take that ya flamer!

TEACHER [*Continues*]: So His plan for me was to be raped at 14 and turn to drugs at the age of 15?

PORN CHUNGTAWUNGA [*From the shadows*]: Was it God's plan to have us "try" this guy and then that one like you might a new cosmetic line that advertises, "Try us for 30 days free!"?

TEACHER [*Continues*]: If God loves us why is there death and poverty, why are there flame wars?

THOMAS OVERPECKER [*From the shadows*]: Wow, this is gay =) Some fools spout out unconstructive trash about someone's work, and that someone gives a damn.

ALICE CHEESEBREW: Maybe you just suck, I mean, getting flamed for every story? Sounds like a factory defect to me.

JEFFERSON: Enough of these images, I can bear no more!

[*Spotlight down on* TEACHER, *up on* JEFFERSON *and* ANGEL.]

ANGEL [*Sparkle noise*]: The glimpse had to be shown, Thomas. Light can still pierce through the darkness of what you have been witness to.

JEFFERSON: Such hatred has never before crossed my path, nor could my greatest imaginations conceive it. There is only one thing needed to do. I will delete my post.

ANGEL [*Sparkle noise*]: I will take you back online, but you will not remember anything about what you have been shown.

JEFFERSON: What? Why would you display these visions to me if I can do nothing about them? I would never have written that post had I known the indescribable consequences. Why won't you let me hinder it from happening?

[ANGEL *turns toward the audience.*]

ANGEL [*Sparkle noise*]:
O heart, the equal poise of love's both parts,
Poetry is like flames,
Big alike with wounds and darts,

Alive in these conquering leaves; alive all the same,
Sparkes, like words on the page,
Walk through all tongues one triumphant flame

We walk abreast, humping our starkness
flame-to-flame, spiraling ever higher
burning holes through turbulent darkness
two hearts pumping passionate fire!

[*Curtain.*]

CHINA 1945-46, KOREA 1950-53, CHINA 1950-53, GUATEMALA 1954, INDONESIA 1958, CUBA 1959-60, GUATEMALA 1960, CONGO 1964, PERU 1965, LAOS 1964-73, VIETNAM 1961-73, CAMBODIA 1969-70, GUATEMALA 1967-69, GRENADA 1983, LIBYA 1986, EL
NOW LET THAT GOLDEN STREAM OF LIGHT FULL OF LOVE AND PEACE AND JOY JUST FLOW OUT FROM YOUR HEART SO THAT IT BECOMES A PART OF THE UNIVERSE...

LYSISTRATA

LYSISTRATA

Performed at Teachers & Writers, New York City, March 6, 2003. Directed by Gary Sullivan, with the following cast:

HEATHER	Jennifer Coleman
BRAD	Gary Sullivan
RADIO	Jennifer Coleman and Gary Sullivan

Scene: HEATHER *and* BRAD, *a young white couple, sit on opposite sides of a table.* BRAD *wears a neck brace.* HEATHER *is on her cell phone.*

HEATHER [*Into phone*]: Liar! You do NOT care about white people! [*Pause.*] Mom. Mom, listen to me. I understand your position. [*Pause.*] Okay. Okay, mom. Okay. [*Pause.*] Well, that's Patti Smith's problem, isn't it? It's not dad's fault—[*Pause.*] Oh, please. Please. Okay. Yeah. *Pause.*] Okay. Yeah. Okay. Mom, I gotta go. Okay, mom. Okay. Yeah. I know. I know. I realize that. Mother, I'm well aware of that. I agree. Yes. I know. I know. I know. I know. You don't have to convince me. I'm with you on that one. I hear ya, mom. Yep. Yep. That's true. Yep. Gotta run now, mom. Yeah. I gotta go. [*Hangs up. To* BRAD, *flirty*:] There's a spider on your cheek. [*Leans over to brush it off.*]

BRAD [*Flinching.*]: Here are the phone numbers for Senators who had originally voted against the War Resolution. Akaka (D)—(202) 224-6361, Bingaman (D)—(202) 224-5521, Boxer (D)—(202) 224-3553, Byrd (D) [*Phone rings.* BRAD *picks up his cell phone.*] Hello? [*Pause.*] Yeah, I know. Because it's fucked up. It's totally fucked up. [*Pause.*] LOOK AROUND, JACK! What do you see but MONOTONY POVERTY and HUMAN MISERY? [*Pause.*] Well, because we are going to make SURE and, and CERTAIN that NO dictator, reactionary force or government TAKES SHIT OVER this time. New Page in the Life of Humanity, Jack! [*Hangs up.*]

HEATHER: Why posture when you can sing of Tuscan?

BRAD: Byrd (D) — (202) 224-3954, Chafee (R)—(202) 224—I need a break. [*Snaps on radio.*]

RADIO:—passes for freedom is, we know only too well, a condition of relative civil liberation based on and expressed principally through the free consumption of commodities—

HEATHER: Boh-ring! [*She switches channels.*]

RADIO:—be a flower of the world, face pointed at the sun, a small gesture of hope, be a different invention, like a flower, learn to use energy that comes from sun and wind, from water and—

[BRAD *switches channels.*]

RADIO:—sham forms of political enfranchisement attendant on that free consumption are possible for us only because they are impossible for the masses of people who spend their lives in poverty and misery working to produce the commodities that we pick and choose—

[HEATHER *switches channels.*]

RADIO:—flowers on rivers, streams, ponds, lakes, harbors, draw flower designs in the sand, dirt, in chalk on sidewalks, draw flowers on post-it notes and stick them—

[BRAD *shuts off radio.*]

BRAD: Read me what you have.

HEATHER [*Picks up page, clears throat.*] "Here are the phone numbers for Senators—"

BRAD: No, before that—

HEATHER [*Throws page down.*] I'm sooo friggin' horny and desperate right now, and this is just NOT helping. Might we look to women's values for a new paradigm?

BRAD: The tragedy is that the television is our only tradition. Quote This window makes me feel like I am outside of the house looking in unquote. Quote This window makes me feel like it's a dictatorship and I don't see any way of getting rid of the city manager unquote. Quote This window makes me feel like—

HEATHER: No, no, no. Listen to me, Brad. My top is green to make the scene, and although I fight, my bottom is white. I'm long and slender, but not real tender, and I certainly am a *fines herbes* member. Some are sweet and cool to eat, but I'm the one who's rolled for fun. If you need some help with your hunches I'm here to inform you I'm sold in bunches. With vitamin C and potassium to spare, one drink of my juice will have your intestines in good repair. What am I?

BRAD: I don't know. Fennel?

HEATHER: [*Makes loud "incorrect buzzer" noise.*]

BRAD: ???

HEATHER: You're not LISTENING to me. LISTEN. In the morning, I like to see children jumping and playing ... a man is feeding pigeons, I like to feel the sunshine ... the birds singing in my window, I like to smell flowers. [*Trying to keep from crying.*] And see, cuz, the energy—sniff—the energy of the flowers DOES feel to me like the energy of the cheeky gazelle, jumping and leaping and prancing. LISTEN TO ME, BRAD! Jumping giraffes, leaping lobsters, prancing pumpkins!

BRAD [*Not convinced.*]: Hibernating hyenas, unhappy hippos ...

HEATHER: Crisply crumbling crackers, clattering clams—

BRAD: Boring bananas, botox, breast-implants, bureaucrats barcoding everybody's genitalia ...

HEATHER: Bouncing banana breads!

BRAD: Disappointing dinosaurs.

HEATHER [*Sighs.*]: Dinosaurs were too cool to have been completely destroyed.

BRAD: They had limited socialization.

HEATHER: Yeah, I had limited socialization when I was a young pup, and now it takes longer for me to trust new people in my life.

BRAD: I used to be very trusting with people, and that's how I got into trouble.

HEATHER: I like people. I'm kind of like Jesus in that way. Except for the miracles. [*Pause.*] Oh! Here's a picture of some of the school children we met in Pahiatua.

BRAD [*Looks briefly at photo, then tosses it aside.*]: I like sheep. [*Reciting.*] "Silly Sally swiftly shooed seven silly sheep. The seven silly sheep Silly Sally shooed shilly-shallied south, to Mrs. Smith's Fish Sauce Shop. These sheep shouldn't slurp fish sauce in a fish sauce shop; shouldn't sheep slurp instead in a shed?"

HEATHER: You don't get it. I'm HORNY.

BRAD: Heather, it's not that I don't respect your position. But when you put salt on an earthworm it burns it up from inside out making it dance, wooble all over the place. People, like the earthworm, are a life form that evolved here on Earth. People, too, must struggle for survival against nature (salt). But we simply cannot turn off our brains, wooble naked into the forest, and survive by instinct. Human beings are the only species that must "figure out" how to survive (i.e. how to build houses, invent vaccines, produce food, etc.). But we must also learn how to nurture our only tool for survival: our MIND (i.e. how to compose inspirational fiction, art, music, speeches, etc.), just like collecting acorns is a perfectly natural required behavior of squirrels. The use of a reasoning mind to manipulate—

[HEATHER'*s phone rings.*]

HEATHER: Hello? [*Pause.*] I'm okay. A little horny. [*Pause.*] Heh, heh, heh! Yeah, definite mind-body split, yeah. He thought the flower language thing was quote undeveloped unquote.

[BRAD'*s phone rings.*]

BRAD: Hello?

HEATHER: Yeah, I know. The language of flowers is totally nuanced and complex! Whereas the Acacia means Friendship or Chaste Love, the Alcea means: I am DEEPLY in love; CONSUMED by love—

BRAD: Are you serious? Well, I'm sorry, but this hardly has anything to do with my "feeling superior."

HEATHER: Belladonna: Silence; Bluebells: Fidelity—

BRAD: Look: it's about generating ideas as a step TOWARDS generating shared opinions as a step TOWARDS doing something about the deep helplessness that we feel right now.

HEATHER: —and they're not all feel-goody, either! The Clematis means: Intelligence or I Love Your MIND—and the evergreen Clematis means: POVERTY! Yeah!

BRAD: And what the hell did you mean by Quote actions are not the domain of aesthetes like yourself unquote? Frankly, your idealism seems little more developed than that of the pacifist to me.

HEATHER: The lotus flower is a symbol for purity. Now, just imagine that beautiful flower growing in your heart. And then imagine a golden stream of light which comes out of the center of that beautiful flower in your heart, and it surrounds you, that golden stream of light, with love and peace.

BRAD: Look: Here's a list of the countries that the U.S. bombed from the end of World War II until the end of the twentieth century, compiled by historian William Blum: China 1945-46, Korea 1950-53, China 1950-53—

HEATHER: Now let that golden stream of light full of love and peace and joy—

BRAD: Guatemala 1954, Indonesia 1958—

HEATHER: just flow out from your heart anywhere and everywhere as far as it will go—

BRAD: Cuba 1959-60, Guatemala 1960—

HEATHER: so that it becomes part of the universe ...

BRAD: Congo 1964, Peru 1965—

HEATHER: And then put yourself into the whole totality of the universe, being part of it, being in it [*holding back the tears*]

BRAD: Laos 1964-73, Vietnam 1961-73, Cambodia 1969-70—

HEATHER: and, and, experiencing the love and the peace and the joy that you yourself have generated there, sniff—

BRAD:
Guatemala 1967-69, Grenada 1983, Libya 1986—

HEATHER: and feel that golden stream of light within you as warmth, light, joy and love! And then—sniff—

BRAD: El Salvador 1980s, Nicaragua 1980s, Panama 1989—

HEATHER: let the golden stream of light go back inside the lotus flower, which closes its petals—

BRAD: Iraq 1991-99, Sudan 1998—

HEATHER: and then anchor this lotus flower, this beautiful, pure flower in your heart, so that it may become one with it. Sniff!

BRAD: Afghanistan 1998, Yugo—hello? Hello? [BRAD *hangs up.*]

HEATHER: I'm sorry. [*Pause.*] No, no, no. I'm sorry, sniff. I'm just horny. Never mind. I'm HORNY. Forget it. I'll call you later. [*Hangs up.*]

[HEATHER *covers her face with her hands. Long pause. She looks up at* BRAD.]

BRAD: Kennedy (D) — (202) 224-4543, Leahy (D) — (202) 224-4242, Levin (D) — (202) 224-6221 — what?

HEATHER: The opposite of war is not peace. The opposite of war is creation. You fuckin' .... CUPCAKE!!!

[*Curtain.*]

MÖEH!
WHAT ABOUT MY POETRY, HUH? MY POETRY IMPLIES ATHEISM?
CUK CUK
DO YOU KNOW HOW HARD I WORK ON THIS SHIT-ASS LANGUAGE? A GUY SHOULD GET A LITTLE RECOGNI-TION, SHOULD-N'T HE?
MEW!
I WROTE THIS NEXT POEM USING REFRIGORATOR MAGNETS. LISTEN:
DIZZZ...
ADAM M.D.
REFRIGORATOR THIEF
CLUB-ING HEADS UNDER MOON
ROB AND YET STOP DEATH NO SLEEP.

PPL IN A DEPOT

PPL IN A DEPOT

Premiered at Small Press Traffic's Poets' Theater Jamboree, San Francisco, January 31, 2003. Directed by Del Ray Cross, with the following cast:

FAITH, an old woman	Stephanie Young
DICK, a con man	Adam Tobin
POLICEMAN	K. Silem Mohammad

Performed again as part of the Flarf Festival, New York City, April 22, 2006. Directed by Stelianos Manolakakis and starring Charles J. Roby (POLICEMAN), Barbara Vann (FAITH), Billy Weimer (DICK).

Scene: *Bus Depot, dawn. A bus pulls in. Doors hiss open.* FAITH, *an old woman carrying a tattered gold handbag, staggers from the door.*

FAITH: Let go of me, Baldilocks, I got GLITTER fever! Cough! Rasberry swirlz ... sody-pop dreams. I'm duckie crazy in the summer bliss of this chocolate bumble bee wonder! This is MY rainbow fantasy, MY star dusted misty hopes. Fuckin' vanilla candles. Red fuckin' tulips, pink fuckin' drink. Quote takes a long hard drag on her cigarette, which has been out since 1976 unquote. Kiwi sparklez ...

DICK [*He wears a white suit covered with graffiti.*]: New in town, right? You got that new-in-town look. Dangerous part of town this time of night for a young lady ... by herself.

FAITH: My kiwi dreams are a crazy monkey with my yummy blue sugar kisses from tootie pop lips.

DICK: Mm-hmm. Lot of people down here try'n take advantage of a situation like that.

FAITH: Well, I got a lot of lilacs.

DICK: In the distance you can see flames rising from a five-gallon drum.

FAITH: Draffidol dreams. [*Belches.*] Alcoholocaust.

DICK: Warm is my middle name.

FAITH [*Extends her hand.*]: Captain Crunch and let's do lunch.

[DICK *reaches out to take her hand. She pulls it away.*]

DICK: I know you. You need money ... and a place to stay.

[*They stare at each other for a moment. DICK starts to take off his jacket.*]

FAITH: You know what the Ass Baboons of Venus tell me?

[*When* DICK*'s jacket is halfway down his arms,* FAITH *blurts out:*]

FAITH: "Anthrapology" will remain spelt like that ... forever!

[FAITH *throws an elbow, smashing* DICK *in the face.* DICK *is stunned.*

FAITH *grabs him and slams against the building.*]

FAITH: And she's on him, hitting him again and—

[POLICEMAN *enters.*]

POLICEMAN: Everything okay here?

FAITH [*Lets go of* DICK *who drops to the ground.*]: Just fine, Ossifer. I started Xenadrine yesterday and noticed a two-pound weight loss but that's only because of the diarrhea.

POLICEMAN: Well, keep me informed, ok? I'll tell you, lots of appetite suppressants are great at first, then they start losing their power—fast.

DICK: I'm up to about 4 Dexatrim Naturals 3X per day and I'm still hungry for at least 500 calories/day.

POLICEMAN: You might have to start switching pills half way thru the bottle from now on.

FAITH: I think all the name brand stuff is a waste of money. They cost a lot more and most of the ingredients don't do anything.

DICK: I take ephedrine and caffeine that I order online—those are the two crucial elements of "stacking."

POLICEMAN: Some people also take aspirin to prevent the body from deactivating the drugs too fast, but there's no proof that works.

DICK: The critical thing is that the E:C ratio is 1:10. Most people take 25 mg E (because it comes in that dose) and 200 mg C.

POLICEMAN: All I understand is blah blah blah blah me horny blah blah blah blah.

FAITH: *Parte ng liriko ng kanta? bakit ang kantang* "I'm horny blah blah blah" *pwedeng patugtugin sa radyo at sa TV?*

POLICEMAN: Ya'll are talented blah blah blah I'm horny blah blah blah who is going steady who is horny blah blah blah. Give me some real conversation! Is anyone CURRENTLY on Stackers?

DICK: I just started taking them yesturday and have had no desire to eat and don't feel hungry at all. I am starting off with taking 1 a day and so far I haven't had any major side affects other than being a little shaky for about 2 hours after I take it. I bought a bottle of 100 capsules at RiteAid for $30. Expensive yes, but worth it if they help me reach my goal.

FAITH: I was on stacker 2's and i loved them but i didn't really lose too much just because i am always up and down in weight and i didnt have that many anyways cause me and my friend split a bottle of 20 for 8 bucks but at gas stations in my town you can get a bottle of stacker 2's for 8 bucks but since i am a bag lady and i am in the southern part of Indiana they dont sell stacker 2's at gas station so praise the lord on this one i have a friend that works at gnc (lol) so he got me a bottle of stacker 3's that comes w/100 capsuls and he gave them to me for 10 bucks yah but they are regular 40 bucks here too damn much for me but i will start them tomorrow and kepp you informed!!!

[FAITH *goes to survey the candy machine.*]

POLICEMAN: I'm not going to eat today, I'm not going to eat tomorrow, and I'm not going to eat the next day ... cuz I'm going to be ... a ... S u p e rmodel! ;)

FAITH: God DAMMIT! [*Smacks the candy machine.*] I don't see ANY cards, NO text OR the Rabbit. Why!??

POLICEMAN: There jus' ain't no convincin' evidence for the existence of God ... He don't exist!

DICK: Then ... what are we ... left with? A buncha ... ELVES?

FAITH [*To* DICK]: I did a search on Yahoo: "I want to kill myself" and your page was the first to pop up. [*Spits on him.*]

DICK: *Ghhaahhgghhh.* [*Holds head in hands.*]

FAITH: "War on terror" makes it sound like we're battling this emotion, and not certain actions. I mean, donkeys leading lions: that's a new one!

POLICEMAN: Yeah, there are a lot of freaky people who do freaky things that are very ... what's the word? Oh, man. Like, a good chunk of them were caused by people who were messed up because of the rye. I've seen all sorts of diagrams and studies and stuff, so I think a lot of it was that. [*Shrugs.*]

FAITH: I honestly think the Rye Bread thing has been overexaggerated. And it's kind of known several Witch Trials where held in areas without the Rye Bread being around. So I ponder the amount of the effects. It doesn't explain why they had thumbscrews and torture. If the Rye Bread did cause anything, it caused the worst that was already in some people to be brought out.

DICK: I sware to GOD ppl are stupid I sware to god ppl are SO stupid like would you WANT to know what it says!!?? God I HATE politics! Why can't we all just play guitars and smoke pot all day? I mean, go read my "Blue skies" poem, it's more concerned with the anarchy of a government running this country than wanting to do our duty and serve the "good old US of A"!

POLICEMAN: That's manly ... Good poem huh? Try something more melancholy: "What makes a man?"

FAITH: You should read my poem to the Queen esp. the crucial info section (a full explanation of how governments should spend and tax locals).

POLICEMAN [*To* FAITH.]: Your poetry is as calming as dawn and most inspiring. I thank you.

FAITH [*To* POLICEMAN]: Your poetry is special because YOU are special.

POLICEMAN: God, your poetry is so amazing! Ecspecially "Fantasy."

FAITH: Your poetry.

POLICEMAN: YOUR poetry.

FAITH: No, YOUR poetry.

POLICEMAN: Girl, you KNOW you're poetry. *winkz*

FAITH: You are a wonderful, unselfish, giving man!

DICK: What about MY poetry? Huh? ... Is that an accurate description of your beliefs? My poetry implies atheism? That I see recurring themes of finality in death? Do you know how hard I work on this shit-ass language?

FAITH: I know how hard you work at being easily dismissible!

DICK: A guy should get a little recognition, shouldn't he? Yeah, so sure I didn't create the world, and I'm not a fallen archangel, and I may not have the hottest body around, but I'm a man (no offense to you femminists out there) who gets the job done. I wrote this poem using refrigorator poetry magnets ... Listen: "Adam MD./ Refrigorator Thief/ Clubing heads under moon/ Rob and yet stop death no sleep."

POLICEMAN [*Clears throat.*]: "On the Death of Allen Ginsberg:
Allen, so far from me,
I such a little circle in your enormity,

the mystery of your hands,
the never-shown in photographs—
suddenly the sunset reeks of you,
the silent dots of streetlights on the road,
fading points of night in the blackness that is
being destinationless.
A little tiny mist of rain falls and I wonder about your friends,
about their ends.
Neal froze to death and Jack?
Jack i don't remember.
You old, still writing, still subtly molding
the fleshscreen of human culture,
still publishing quietly, interviewing with
Vin Scelsa, still loving? Dying.
Jack Kent Cooke died too and he got a front-page
spread in the Washington Post and a spot on
the local news.
I cut out your obituary it didn't have a picture.
Allen you were not so old. Seventy is
not a good stopping place. My grandma
still played tennis at seventy. You
lived on the Lower East Side.
I was in New York this weekend,
sleeping while you died. Not so far from you;
my first time in the city, your last.
Driving home, crying, I remembered most of that part at
the end of Sunflower Sutra, but I
misquoted a bit—not many things
are perfect in this world—your words
were one.
Never did i dream your words would outlive you.
You were meant to exist. I don't
know how to be you, I can't
replace you. Dream your poetry,
spring rain, a knock on my
door. Opportunity, the hand
of the dead."

[*Curtain.*]

RINGU

RINGU

Jill
Jane
Tim
Daria
Yusaku

They sit in cubicles wearing headsets.

JILL: Um-hm ... ring ring ring ring "Uh ... Er ... is this mister @?"

JANE: Yeah ... BEING ADDED (THUMP). Oh ... (EMBARRASSED) Well, I... um ... er, that is, I, uh ... is, I, ah ... hm.

TIM: How's the guy situation? So, how — how's the ... they're not ... brother and sister?

DARIA: ... you know? Oh yeah ... you know ... yeah ... it was a joke, yeah. *BLUSH*

YUSAKU (sweat drop): Ah, well. Happy cute things to, uh ...

TIM: Um ... guys? How is it ...

JILL: Lit up? Mmmhmmm mmmhmmm ... ah, yes ... easy for a man of his, er ...

DARIA: Ah! ah-ha! ay! ay-yi-yi!

JANE: Yeah, vitriolic wings ... vitriolic wings ... er ... but with vitriolic wings, um ... seems ... to ... uh ...

YUSAKU (worried glance): ... well yeah Larry, uh ... (laughs) you're, uh ... very, uh ... "I like old people."

DARIA: <Disconnect>, oh ... 09:27, <Disconnect>, ah. ... 14:55, <Disconnect>, er ... 17, <Disconnect>, huh ... 30:42, <Disconnect>, uh ... yeah ...

JILL: ... at my ass? You cracked — ah ... You think I need you? Uh ... Oh, and if you ... tied to the bed?

TIM: The Leaves are falling again ... *wakes up* ... Huh?

JANE: ... to use sandpaper on your uh ... ah ... the front of the bus? Oh ... *nervous laughter* uh, yeah... the whole, um, foreordained destiny ...

YUSAKU: It's ah ... not my ... ah, "English duck," huh ...

JANE: This is hell? Yeah, well, um, Pardone moi ... Yeah ...

TIM: ... faded ... flowers? Yes, um ... I ... uh... and little twirly bits and — yeah ...

JILL: All of you?? ... You mean you already...? Uh-huh ... So — is that anger?

YUSAKU: My fake ... er ... no, I CAN, ah, WOMEN ... uh ... "fabric of the sand" ...

DARIA: Oh shit ... I need to find clothes ... yeah that means keeeee ... um ...

JANE: Yeah, that did a lot of good. Oh... huh? ... Um ... (chuckles) Huh huh hua! Oh, le persefalge!

JILL: HicanIhelpyou? HAHAHAHAHAHAHA-HAAAAAAAAAAAA! Jeronimoooo, yeah ...

TIM: Oh, I bet he remembers you, the ... um ... octopus ...

YUSAKU: *cocks eyebrow* Um ... Ah-ban-eh-bee-ah ... OMG, yeah <aberrant> huh

JILL: <aberrant> ah ... 14:55 <aberrant> hm ... 14:56 <aberrant> oh ... 14:57 <aberrant> um ... 14:57 <aberrant> er ...

DARIA: Huh-huh-huh! ... Oh, er ... yes, but, er ... HUH! But ... um, OH ... Hm ... Never mind ...

TIM: Hey! I'm trying to brighten your day here motherfucker ...

JILL: I found cereal — yeah! ... and is more polite than "Huh ... Oh, well, I'm married ... (Except, uh, this year ... (Um — er ...

YUSAKU (furrowing his brow): Hm ... Uh, what else it say ... fuckin' ... knowin'-self, hm ... just so empty, huh ...

JANE: Yeah ... THE, the uh uh ...

TIM: Um, hi ...

JILL: Ah ...

YUSAKU: Hm ...

JANE: Er ... yeah ... MYSELF (thinking quickly)

JILL: Um, yeah, because, uh

JANE: ... me to send him my, um, panties and, my, um ...

DARIA: Alright then; no panties ... It's different look I have now, and I think ...

JILL: Ugh ... absolutely ... I got some secret items I can't ...

YUSAKU: wouldn't appreciate me discussing sniffing panties ...

JANE: He'd look at all the women ... UGH! ... No more angry testicles. I'll just whip off my panties and ... Ooh, look! ... Oh, and you know I ... shirt contest!

DARIA: ... I'm workin' the polka dot panties ... looks good if you've got ... ugh ugh ugh I'm like okay ... day u look and see no ... the area so flat — oh well, it doesn't look ...

TIM: Have you got any pets?" (Ugh ... nop [Brain13] what do u look ... older so thats why [GrnHeLL] oh ... [GrnHeLL] panties? ... nickname] [The Reg] so, u got ... [Dennis] no i wanted ...

YUSAKU: ... I have no idea how I got ... ugh ...

JANE: ... ass is mine for two minutes ... has shoved those panties ...

JILL: Look, just shut up, click on the ... 2am and I'm in no ... but tonight, oh-hoh, tonight is ...

DARIA: Went Saucy In My Panties ... 03/07/01 ... I love, two pairs of pants, cute bra/panties sets ...

TIM: ... Try the panties," he said. ... Ugh! ... look ... he knew Martine spoke no English ...

JANE: ... I'll go! (Ugh.) So anyway ... showing the "You've Got ... They're very nice panties" UHHH OH ... And I look down to ...

YUSAKU: ... pans to Alicia in her space panties ... if you don't want to look ... oh, yes, I love it ...

JILL: These panties ... Have you got a minute ... Hello, I must say these panties ... Okay, it appears as though no ... holds aloft a pair of ...

TIM: ... think it's time you got your panties ... I mean, look ...

DARIA: I had no idea I even ordered this ... they all look the same oh ...

YUSAKU: ... wearing nothing but a bra and panties ... and out stepped a ...

TIM: BRA. Oh my love, I've ... PANTIES. (Pure joy.) AAAAAH! ... Right ON, then, you get your panties ...

JANE: Ugh ... snakes ... panties ... you can masturbate now ...

JILL: "Oh, customer, we'll dance for you. Feel free to touch anything you wish."

DARIA: "Hol... Hold on, you guys... So, Sora-san, surely you don't approve of this ...!"

YUSAKU: "Hmph!! Males cannot be The Outdone. Hmph!" (Stars sripping.)

TIM: "Sora-san?!" Ugh... my head! (Bras land on him.) "Wahhh! (Panties follow) Gu...guys, stop this! I'm... I'm no of yet, please!"

JILL: "Oh — it's okay to. Everyone is being bald."

DARIA: All of their crotches... They swing and I see things ... I don't believe it at all ... Oka... Oka... oka....

JANE: "What's the matter, Masahiko-kun? Hurry and get undress, everyone!"

TIM: "Oh my."

YUSAKU: So-Sora-san's chest looks like a woman's, and the thing at his crotch ... Isn't there!

DARIA: All ... you ... naked ... fucking ... inside ... oh shit. OH SHIT... la-la-la-la-la ... OH JESUS GOD IN HEAVEN FUCK FUCK FUCK ... I'm coming ...

JANE: ... Oh god, oh god, it's true, you ... We're coming now this ... that meets folk, watch your leg there, oh ... Hannah, I'm called Hannah. ... I feel like ...

JILL: I'm coming now ... Oh my God, baby, I'm fucking your ass, your big, tight white ass, bitch! Harder! ...

TIM: ... multiple orgasms. ... I come so many times, I ... a little, but everything feels so ... you are coming and I'm coming ... a major good time, oh god ...

DARIA: ... dear ... so yelling "Oh, God," "Yes!" or almost ...

YUSAKU: ... up I want my rockets many ... think you are me cuz I'm mad ... you I'm coming, like ... "your dog" ... seem so ... orgasms ...

JANE: I ... swells were ... our body coming ... I gasp, calling our "Oh God ..."

JILL: Oh ... Oh God, Oh God of an orgasmic simulator ... oh ... well boys, I offer some ... I be you coming ... fuck me ...

TIM: So uh ... yeah ... I ... you ...

DARIA: Um? disregard that last sentence ? there is a rather large ...

JILL: *Sniff* I feel so ... *sniff* ...

YUSAKU: ... anyway, let me give you a massage ... I mean ... um ... uh ... er ... uh ... I must go ...

[*A long pause.*]

JANE: God, I am SOOOOO embarrassed ...

[*A long pause.*]

TIM: Whoa ... to love one-another. This is not ... we all know people make such ... use them, and most of all ... Feelings: Whoa oh oh, Feeeelings ...

JANE: Whoa-whoa-whoa! ... I am NOT ... uh ... gotta get the wording right and all ... uh ... I'm not even gonna comment on it ...

[*A long pause.*]

JILL: Well, but anyways, I gotta jet now... (joy, lol)

DARIA: I'ma pretty darn busy person, too. I'll ... uh ... check back!! Later!!

YUSAKU: Goodbyes make me fucking sick. Anyway, I gotta jet, girl's comin over, I gotta Bush to work on.

JANE: Yeah, I'm just not into ... stuff right now ... xx im really bored lol really ok, so we see you later ahhuh, see you people later

TIM: Until next time lol I sound like that rainbow haha peace!

YUSAKU: Bye for now ... Happy tripping and Keep it rolling!

[*A long pause.*]

DARIA: Sorry for not adding anything else.

[*A long pause.*]

JANE: What is the, uh ...

[*A long pause.*]

YUSAKU: Cough! "Sotto voce"

JANE: ... the, uh, the word ...

[*Pause.*]

TIM: ... could someone ... hand me ... my ...

YUSAKU: Yeah, uh ... I dunno ... Scratch ... I guess ... Scratch Scratch ... it just seems so...

[*A long pause. A phone rings and continues to ring until the end of the play.*]

JILL: Riiing!

JANE: Riiiing... Riiing... Riiing...

YUSAKU: Riiing... Riiing... Riiing... Riiiing... Riiing...

DARIA: Riiing... Riiing... Riiing... Riiing...

TIM: Riiiing... Riiing... Riiing... Riiing... Riiing... Riiing... Riiiing... Riiing... Riiing... Riiing... Riiing...

JILL: Riiing Riiing ... riiing riiing!

JANE: RIIING, RIIING!!

YUSAKU: *beep* *beepbeepbeepbeepbeepbeepbeepbeep* *riiing*

DARIA: Riiiing... riiing... riiing... riiing... riiing... riiing... riiiing... riiing...

TIM: RIIING! Hello? RIIING!

JANE: “Riiing! Riiing! Riiing!”

TIM: ~Riiing~Riiing~Riiing~ “Hello?”

YUSAKU: Hello ... Riiing~Riiing~Riiing~ Hello? Hello ...

DARIA: Riiing, riiing, riiing...

JILL: RIIING !!!!.tick .... RIIING!! ... tick. RIIING .... tick .... RIIING ....tick.

TIM: Riing, riiing...

JANE: “Riiing, riiing.” “Riiing, riiing.”

DARIA: RIIING,RIIING,RIIIING,RIIING.

YUSAKU: Riiing < >ring < >riiing < >ring < >“Unh, hello?”

JILL: Riiing! Riiiing! ... Riiing! Riiiing! Riiiing! ...

JANE: “Hello?”

YUSAKU: <beep beep beep beep beep beep beep> <beep beep beep, beep beep beep, beep beep beep beep>

DARIA: *riiiing*riiing*

JILL: AOOG ... AOOGAOOGAOOO ... hello?

TIM: BREEP, RRIIINNNNGGG, hello? RRRRIINNNNGGG ... VOOT!

YUSAKU: Hello? Hello? CHIK, CLAK, KLIK, SHRIIIING!

JANE: DING DING! Hello!

DARIA: CHAK, gugk. Hello? SWASHHH-THUP ... VZZZT ... VZZZZT ... VZZZZZZZZZZZT

JILL: BEOW!

JANE: THWIP!

TIM: FSHSSSTTT ...

YUSAKU: BZZZ!

DARIA: FZZZZL, GZZZT ... hello?

JANE: KKKKRRRRRAAAAAKKKKKLLLL

TIM: KKKRAKKKKLL, KRAKKKL, KRAKKL, KRAKKLL, KRRAKKLLL

YUSAKU: Hello? KZAKK. Hello?

DARIA: KZAT; KZZZAT; PRZZAT; RRZZTTT; SHZZZZT; SVASH

JILL: Hello? SZIT

YUSAKU: TZZZZTT ... ZAPT!

JANE: ZRASH!

TIM: ZZRAAK!

DARIA: Hello?

JANE: ZZRAK-ZZRAKK

YUSAKU: ZZRAKSHHHHH

JILL: ZZRARKT; hello? ZZRRAKKK; HELLO?

TIM: HELLO??? ZZWWAKT!

DARIA: ZZZRAKK-ZZZRATCH!

YUSAKU: ZZZT; hello?

JANE: ZZZT ...

TIM: Zzzt ...

JILL: zzz ... hello? ... t-t-t ...

TIM: t-t-t ...

YUSAKU: t-t-t ...

JANE: t-t-t ...

DARIA: t-t ...

JILL: t ... hello?

TIM: t ...

YUSAKU: t ...

JANE: t ...

[*Curtain.*]

GRAY MATTER

GRAY MATTER
for Stan Apps

Performed for the Segue Series at Bowery Poetry Club, New York City, February 4, 2006. Directed by Gary Sullivan, with the following cast:

JENNY, a VJ	Sharon Mesmer
DEWEY, a rap artist	Jim Behrle

Scene: *They are on television.*

JENNY: I sat on this for a bit because I didn't wanna bring any undue tension to you in lieu of Tuesday's tragedy. I'm talking about your album cover. It depicts a giraffe holding a detonator blowing up the World Trade Center.

DEWEY: When my daughter was little, she was terrified of giraffes and we didn't know why. We finally figured out that every time she heard someone say to shut a window because a draft was coming in, she thought a giraffe was trying to get into the house!

JENNY: Seriously, man: In a new Mariah Carey song a rapper says 3 keys, 8 hammers, lobster shrimp. Several other references to "shrimp and go." What does this mean? Checked rap dictionaries—no reference.

DEWEY: "To shrimp" means to suck on someone's toes in order to give or receive sexual gratification. "Shrimp and go" is what I think it takes to make a revolution. I definitely espouse revolution and overthrowing the system. So that a topless bar could mean everyone has to be topless (men and women).

JENNY: If you think America is so bad, why not leave and go to another place?

DEWEY: When people say you aren't patriotic, it's usually white or European Americans. While on a car journey with my grandparents when I was about six my Nan told me you could tell how much milk a cow had inside them just by looking at how white they were. So obviously a cow that was mostly white was due for milking.

JENNY: When I was little, I believed that hamburger and steaks and pretty much all meat in general came from a cow. Only, I believed that somehow the cow chose to give it away, kind of like milking a cow, but more friendly. I think I even had an image in my head of a cow talking to a farmer, saying "OK, you can take a little off my belly for hamburgers today." I thought cows were so thoughtful; and I cried when I found out that that's not how it works.

DEWEY: A lot of people don't know that Kuwait used to belong to Iraq and it was America and Britain that separated them. That's where you get BP gas stations which is British Petroleum Gas ... also your boy Noriega in Panama. He was part of the CIA.

JENNY [*Raising her hand.*]: I for one plead guilty to still getting off on "Rap Declares War" (a collaborative venture featuring seminal funkologists War with the southland's brown cream, most notably Kid Frost, A.L.T. and A Lighter Shade of Brown)! [*Laughter.*] Seriously, tho. When listening to last year's hit "Because I Got High," words like "deep" and "enigmatic" don't usually come to mind. But upon further examination, the words make sense: Many a blunt has been lit and a bong been hit as the familiar bass line kicks in.

DEWEY: Smoking weed is cool, and I fully love doing it.

JENNY: Yeah, but what happens: I was talking to you about "big, hairy yaks" and you said, "Hairy? You mean feathery, don't you?" After a few quick questions it turned out you thought a Yak was a big gray bird.

DEWEY: The most effective lie, according to Cees Hamelink is a gray lie. A gray lie contains an element of truth or assumptions that cannot be verified. Until I was eight or nine I thought you could tell venomous and non-venomous snakes apart based on the simple fact that poisonous snakes can talk.

JENNY: So? I used to believe llamas had two heads!

DEWEY: See, this really is a colony. The thing about moving to another country is that the U.S. is running the whole wide world. It would not help at all to move anywhere else.

JENNY: I would just add that anyone who has what we may consider an informed perspective step it up a notch and involve themselves in this ongoing discussion by writing or calling to keep these perspectives out there so people don't fall prey to only what is being handed down by mass media.

DEWEY: It's obvious the corporate media is structured in a way that protects and furthers the interests of state-corporate power in the absence of any conspiracy, or even overt interference. You grow up believing that the people on TV can see you and so you don't do anything.

JENNY: I used to believe that I was constantly being filmed by a secret hidden camera. I always tried to look my best and not to pick my nose ... just in case!

DEWEY: I've gotten emails from people who were soooo mad that I would put out such a cover ... with or without a giraffe. People just believe that everyone is constantly being filmed. This is due largely to crime reconstruction programs. But people should be mad that the U.S. has used the death of these people at the World Trade Center to beef up the military and to further oppress people not only here but all around the world.

JENNY: Like, if you hit the TV with a hammer and the screen breaks then whatever you were watching might come out of the TV. When I was very little, I thought that TV shows "stayed inside the TV" until it was turned on. When we watched TV, the shows were "leaking out." When I started going to school, I would come home in the afternoon, try to watch "Sesame Street" and find that it wasn't on. I then asked Mom not to watch TV while I was at school, as it "wasted" "Sesame Street."

DEWEY: That's the interesting thing about propaganda. The old tricks still work the best. [*Clears throat.*] You have a ring of yellow flowers and a ring of white and a ring of blue and so they are on television and on radio and everything and they are sorting the blocks they used to complete the flower picture into their favorite television shows and the time they were on television b/c they're a sacred cow when on television or related to flowers on a flat trailer being pulled by a car like a float with flowers for example, in the illustrations, the ground and the flowers soak up puddles of rain portrayed as characters as they are on television in time to music hanging in baskets on television and in magazines the economy and its flower, civilization, who are there with Valentines and flowers for the veterans, depicted as if they were on television or in movies, newspapers, magazines, like egg cartons cut up into individual cups—

[*Long, uncomfortable pause.*]

JENNY: I used to believe that nobody loved me, and that everybody was taking advantage of me. That's when I got involved in a team of 120 people who lived the life of the heavy metal music in sin and uncleanness. I could not sleep at night. I thought that somebody was next to me, and wanted to take my soul.

DEWEY: Why do educated people believe in demons? I can't fathom this. I have absolutely no idea why you would believe in demons.

JENNY: Well, I think because it's fashionable, it's crazy, and you have to let your hair down sometimes. I used to think our house was haunted, so every time I had to go to the bathroom in the night, I would drape a blanket over my head and shuffle toward the bathroom going: "Wooh, wooh!"

DEWEY: Yeah, but your education should have covered this, or you should have applied enough of your education to come to this realization. Maybe it would have to be inspected on a case-by-case basis to get to the bottom of it.

JENNY: Empirical evidence is not enough to claim that a function is biologically determined—

DEWEY: But if belief is genetic, it's influenced by multiple genes acting simultaneously. With the recent completion of the human genome project, it may eventually be possible to find a belief gene or two.

JENNY: Well, here's what I believe: I believe rap involves brains, talent, skill and imagination, and to make it truly art, heart—even if it's very angry heart. Still ... are rappers really like they are on television?

DEWEY: For the most part, yes. In the short term, they're easy to switch on and off. Sometimes that thing is only the thoughts in my own head.

[*Curtain.*]

THE MEDIUM

THE MEDIUM

JOEL, a medium
GINA, a medium
ROBERT, a medium
GHOSTVOICE 1
GHOSTVOICE 2
GHOSTVOICE 3

Scene: JOEL, GINA *and* ROBERT *sit around a circular table. Their arms are outstretched on the tables, palms pressed to the table tops.*

JOEL: Wait ... I'm getting something ... MAMMA MIA! The official site for the worldwide production of the smash hit musical based on the songs of ABBA.

GINA: ABBA Punk As Fuck Riot Grrrl.

ROBERT: In the Vilna Ghetto and in the Rudninkai Forest (both in Lithuania), Abba Kovner, only 25 years old, led resistance fighters against the murderous Nazi enemy.

JOEL: If punk was good for killing Abba and Fleetwood Mac, why do punk fans always say how great it was that it killed bands such as Yes, Rush and Genesis?

GINA: It was like that essay Lester Bangs once wrote about punk, and who invented it.

ROBERT: Interestingly enough, the word "Abba" occurs strikingly early and in a wide range of first-century "Christian" texts, all of which were written in Greek. Both Mark and Paul took pains in their text to translate "Abba" as "father."

JOEL: Many former punk and New Wave artistes later admitted to levels of fondness and respect for ABBA they were unwilling to own up to in their early years.

GINA: Abba Kovner was one of the greatest poet-fighters in the Jewish tradition. He was a hero to us all, and a splendid poet. To read, hear, experience the intimacy of his last months—that is something very powerful.

ROBERT: So "Abba," then, is the first prayer fragment that all major scholars agree can be traced with reasonable certainty back to this historical Jesus. I find no reason to doubt this conclusion.

JOEL: Except that the true pop ideal is faceless, has no politics, has no significant history or widespread mythology, in fact, has no significant legacy at all outside the music itself. It is a consummate chameleon — a ruthless, efficient, unstoppable machine.

[*The lights suddenly go out. Mysterious* GHOSTVOICES *are heard.*]

GHOSTVOICE 1: Hoooooow caaan yoooooooou criticiiiiiiiiiii-ize Rooooobot Chickeeeeeeen when you haaaaaaaaaaaaaven't even seeeeeeeeeeeen Robooooooooot Chiiiiiiicken?

GHOSTVOICE 2: Roooobot Chickeeeeeen is amaaaaaaaaaaaaaaaaziiiiing

GHOSTVOICE 3: Yoooooooou shouuuuuuld WAAAAAAAAATCH Rooobot Chickeeeeeen befoooooooore poooooooooooosting thaaaaat shiiiiiiiit, maaaan

[*Pause. Then lights come back up.* MEDIUMS *as before.*]

JOEL: I always tell the Karaoke Queen that Elton John was the death of rock and roll. His emphasis on Las Vegas style shows with a gay edge effectively ended the great era of rock and roll. Rock was, and should be, a macho phenomenon. The gayification of rock seemed like fun, but it was fatal.

GINA: Donald, your story is somewhat similar to mine. I enjoyed pop music a lot in the early to mid 70s. In 76, the year I graduated from high school, I noticed that there weren't as many "really great" songs as there had been in the few previous years. I remember my friends and I talking about this.

ROBERT: Is there some reason to ignore the elephant in the parlor here—namely, age?

JOEL: Not true. Jars of Clay, Amy Grant, Sixpence None the Richer, dc Talk, and MxPx (among others) have all had significant radio hits. And none of them had to hide their faith to get their songs played.

ROBERT: P.O.D. is a good example of how the Christian music industry can actually HOLD BACK talented artists.

JOEL: In today's world, I believe the word "Christian" is often simply a marketing term used to describe products and services—it's not necessarily indicative of a lifestyle modeled after Jesus Christ.

GINA: Christians have a hope the world needs. But that hope must reflect the reality of our human journey in a fallen world. When it does the culture listens and its trajectory is challenged.

ROBERT: Abba/Father—Luke preserves the earlier form while Matt expands it.

[*The lights go down again.* GHOSTVOICES.]

GHOSTVOICE 1: Thaaaat shit is soooooooooooooo baaaaaaaaaaaaked

GHOSTVOICE 2: Baaaaaaaaaaaaaaaaaaaaaked

GHOSTVOICE 1: Sooooooooooooo baaaaaaaaaaaaaaaked

GHOSTVOICE 3: Pooootaaaaaaaatoooooes … claaaaaaaaaaaaaamssss …

GHOSTVOICE 2: Baaaaaaaaaaaaaaaaaaaaaaaaaaaaaaaked

[*The lights come back up.* MEDIUMS *as before.*]

JOEL: Tony remarks on his blog how Abba seems to operate as a catalyst for discussion around other "agendas." He suggests that Abba, an Aramaic term, was Jesus' special way of addressing God with filial intimacy.

GINA: I propose a new definition of pop music: "Any music in any style that prompts our Creator to say, 'Well done.'"

ROBERT: Now that "The Passion of the Christ" is out on video, I was desiring some input from the board into the approximate age that some of you would deem appropriate to view the feature?

GINA: Well, you can't fully understand a contemporary work of art or pop culture unless you know at least something about its heritage.

JOEL: Top Ten Things that Calvin edited out of his Institutes just before publication of the 1536 edition: 10. Indulgent reference to King Francis I as a "Wine-swilling little Popemeister." 9. Dustjacket endorsement from J.I. Packer ...

ROBERT: I was at the mall today in Tampa ... at a BOSE store buying some headphones. The BOSE employees pointed out the famous rocker, Gene Simmons of KISS, in the store directly across—Victoria's Secret. I found it quite sad. He is all about the here and now—sex, money etc.

GINA: People think Gene Simmons is an asshole b/c he's too rich and has too many chicks, and people like that are big targets. Donald Trump and Hugh Hefner, they're both friends of mine; I like them as human beings, and I know who they really are. But to anyone on the street: "Man, that guy's got a billion dollars ... he's an asshole."

ROBERT: I wanted to ask him something different, because he must get asked the same things all the time.

GINA: I have been thinking a lot lately about why people want to be famous and why they want to run around after famous people. The thing that really irritates the famous, is the way they get spotted and folks ask for autographs or stalk them and other wierd things like hanging around airports just to see famous people, or going through their garbage. What does such behaviour denote?

ROBERT: Well, ABBA singer Agnetha Faltskog has admitted that fame drove her to become a recluse.

GINA: So that then gives people "the right" (in their view) to stalk her, ring her home, find her address, and hang about in places where she might just show up?

JOEL: Celebrities often complain about not being able to walk in the street, go in high street shops, or do other commonplace things that ordinary people do, as they would be mobbed and would feel threatened or insecure in some way.

ROBERT: Faltskog didn't sing at all for 13 years. She didn't even have a hi-fi at home. She developed a microphone phobia, and had visions that fans grabbed hold of her, or that she was being suffocated by the sheer weight of people.

[*The lights go down again.* GHOSTVOICES.]

GHOSTVOICE 1: Faaaaaaaaaaaame is fleeeeeeeeeeeeting. Stuuuuuuuuupidity is eteeeeeeeeeeeeeeernal

GHOSTVOICE 2: Straaaaaaaaaaaange to be knooooooooown and yet be soooooooo looooooonelyyyyyyy

GHOSTVOICE 3: Faaaaaaame is a vaaaaaaapooooor

[*Lights up.* MEDIUMS.]

GINA: Ahh, the ears. What wonderful instruments. God's satellite dishes, direct to our mind. They take in a complex myriad of sound waves, sort them out, and feed them to the brain for processing. When the brain processes the signals from pop music they can produce profound emotions and feelings. They can spur memories and thoughts, and they can affect your spirit and your soul.

JOEL: Beautiful poem and so true. Hugs!

ROBERT: But you're reacting just like anyone else! You're not a moderator. Pop music is actually *worse* than anti-Semitic poetry.

JOEL: "Poetry is news that stays news" (Ezra Pound).

GINA: And it was Ezra Pound, above all, who made ours an age of translation: Celan, Abba Kovner, Nelly Sachs ...

ROBERT: But what scope is intended in that series?

GINA: Bible translation is like that. Translators can be in awe of the fact that they are dealing with God's Word. They feel that if they are standing between God's Word and the Christian public, they've got to be sure they get it right. So they go looking for something safe.

JOEL: Once, in a Paris bookstore, I turned to the shelves that house literature in translation, and took down some volumes of Wordsworth and Yeats in French. Reading The Prelude's measured lines, with their Racinian metre and the rhetorical temper so congenial to the French language, I could discover nothing of Wordsworth's own poetic manner; the laconic, even tedious voice had been imbued with a resonance totally absent in the original.

ROBERT: Failing to grapple with the meaning in context is just as much an interpretation as adding information that is not fully explicit. And this has nothing to do with political correctness or hypersensitivity regarding the Holocaust. Or theology for that matter. This is a straight up question about author's intended reference.

GINA: Abba. Twista. The Beatles. Expertise: taking over the world ... one smile at a time.

[*Curtain.*]

WRITTEN IN STYROFOAM

WRITTEN IN STYROFOAM

DAVID MOORHEAD, editor of *Tempo*
SHIRLEY WOOD, a blogger
BARISTA

Time and place: 2007. In line at the café.

DAVID MOORHEAD [*Thinking aloud*]: OMG, I am totally falling in love with Brooke. How can I tell her that I killed her daughter?

SHIRLEY WOOD [*Shaking her head at the book in her hands*]: You have to be in the mood for some death-defying Orwellian back-flips to read "Poems From Guantánamo."

DAVID MOORHEAD: I am such a tard when it comes to Brooke! It's because I respect her values too much. [*To* BARISTA:] Hey, is my iced frappuccino and my muffin ready yet?

BARISTA: Just one second. [*To* SHIRLEY:] You know, the bulk of those poems are so vague and conventional, they might have been written at any point in history by anyone suffering anything.

DAVID MOORHEAD [*To* BARISTA]: Hey, wait a minute. I know you.

BARISTA: I don't think so.

SHIRLEY WOOD: It's chilling, isn't it, when even poetry is shackled, gagged, and tortured?

DAVID MOORHEAD: Yeah, yeah, I saw you on "The Wave." You're a real babe, you know that? There is no way I would have backed off like your lame boyfriend did.

BARISTA: Look, why don't I just get you your frappuccino and you leave me alone, ok?

DAVID MOORHEAD: Been left alone too much. That's your problem.

SHIRLEY WOOD: The Times review of "Poems from Guantánamo" left me with the impression that what is not in the book and why it is not in the book are at least as germane as what is.

BARISTA: Allowing a voice for the voiceless sounds more like ad copy than a call for justice.

DAVID MOORHEAD: I don't think so. I think you need some "special attention."

BARISTA: I think I need you to get out of my face.

SHIRLEY WOOD [*To* DAVID MOORHEAD]: May I join you? Because I just had the most brilliant inspiration, and it came from reading the latest issue of your magazine.

DAVID MOORHEAD: You read "Tempo"?

[*They make their way to a table.*]

SHIRLEY WOOD: Religiously. And I was particularly fascinated with the latest issue, your profiles on the Guantánamo poets.

DAVID MOORHEAD: Those profiles ripped a giant hole in Brooke and my relationship. But I hope to be closing it just a little. The pain will always there. But when I'm with Brooke, there is peace and hope and even joy. I think that she feels it, too.

SHIRLEY WOOD: "T'was brillig
and the slithy toves
did gyre and gimble in the wabe
all whimsy were the borogroves
and the mome raths outgrabe"

DAVID MOORHEAD: What does that have to do with anything?

SHIRLEY WOOD: Oh, come on. A book produced by the Pentagon? A book of "bad" poetry by "bad" people? The poems are actually being put into their OWN form of Guantánamo.

DAVID MOORHEAD: I wonder if al-Qaeda plans to put out any of Daniel Pearl's haiku, or the sonnets of Nicholas Berg. [*Pause.*] Oh! A shiver just went right through me, and it was like Brooke was suddenly here.

BARISTA [*Bringing their order to the table*]: When Foucault wrote that the "author" is a product of the discourses of her times, he could as well have included the reader. "Who reads?"

SHIRLEY WOOD: It's easy enough to figure out "who is reading" in most cases, by the reader's response.

DAVID MOORHEAD [*Standing, walking slowly toward edge of stage*]: Oh, I get it, Brooke. You want to play "Phantom of the Opera"? Okay. We're all alone, and I'm in the mood for a singing lesson. I'm going to sing now. I hope no one comes up behind me to ravage me. I feel a mysterious presence. Who is it?

SHIRLEY WOOD: I find the claim that this book shouldn't be taken seriously, "certainly not as poetry," to be extraordinary. Why should it not be taken seriously?

BARISTA: Firstly, most of these poems, as I understand the situation, were not written by poets, they were scraped into Styrofoam cups with pebbles. To take them seriously is like a cosmologist taking the Book of Genesis seriously.

SHIRLEY WOOD: "When I heard pigeons cooing in the trees,/ Hot tears covered my face."

DAVID MOORHEAD: There are times I would really love to hear these poems explode into a different kind of jam, looser and free of the constant drama. [*Going back to the table.*] I'm not tanking the book over this, I'd just love to hear these poets go NUTS with less of the lamenting.

SHIRLEY WOOD: It's one thing to drop a word like "Diet Coke" or something into a poem, but to repeatedly use language that a normal person would never say or use?

BARISTA [*Heading back to the counter*]: This book has so many OMFG moments it's hard to assemble highlights.

SHIRLEY WOOD: The big realization that I had is how much this book totally relates to blogging: You are more attractive when you share, share, share yourself.

DAVID MOORHEAD: But blogging isn't about hand-picking shiny, happy comments for display purposes. It's about conversation and meaningful dia—

SHIRLEY WOOD [*Interrupting*]: I think blogging will pass as a fad simply because most bloggers don't know what they are talking about, don't care about real truth. Most are just windbags with an ax to grind.

DAVID MOORHEAD [*Stands on the table, hands on hips*]: After six years of successful blogging I have decided to title myself "Supreme Blogger Extraordinaire." That's the great thing about owning a blog, you can say whatever you want—it's your blog! [*Begins kicking the coffee cups and muffins off the table.*]

SHIRELY WOOD: Isn't that true with poetry?

[BARISTA *places high-speed fan on counter and aims it at* DAVID MOORHEAD.]

DAVID MOORHEAD: But most poetry written today is not ecstatic. Most 21st century poetry casts an ironic gaze over a terribly violent landscape, and exhales a seen-it-all sigh, or a shudder, or a well-placed kick. [*Kicks the last muffin off the table.*]

[BARISTA *turns the fan on high.*]

DAVID MOORHEAD [*Orating, hair flying in the fan's wind*]: Indeed, the world is a frightening place! [*Unbuttons shirt.*] And so I am interested in reading poetry that finds its vigor in uncertainty, and that still strives, through its grieving, to delight its reader with language! [*Throws shirt on floor, begins to unzip his pants.*] That, to me, is one of the greatest things about poetry: it is a sensual and cerebral pleasure!

SHIRLEY WOOD: Is this supposed to feel good or something?

BARISTA [*Sarcasm*]: Wait till he gets to your shoulder blades. You'll see God.

DAVID MOORHEAD [*Pants around ankles*]: The mystery and enigmas of poetry have no place in the framework of Islamic law! "The Qur'an is in truth the revelation of God, and the utterance of a noble messenger. It is no poet's speech!"

[BARISTA *holds Styrofoam cup in front of fan for a moment, then lets go, sending cup missile-like toward* DAVID MOORHEAD. *Repeats this, punctuating the following speech.*]

DAVID MOORHEAD: I believe poetry readers are the most sensual of readers and by that I mean they not only read and appreciate the words – they feel them! [*Cup launch.*] I believe poetry should be a refuge from the utter and base ugliness which so often surrounds us, and a safe haven from the tempest of daily life! [*Cup launch.*] In fact, I believe poetry is an art and therefore has only one central purpose, to provide us with verbal beauty! [*Cup launch.*] The term "performance poet," however, has never appeared on my biography, b/c I believe poetry must work as well on the page as it does the stage! [*Cup launch.*] My favorite Chaffin quote is, "I believe poetry is often an outlet for those who suffered a pre-verbal developmental insult." Good for you, C. E. Chaffin! [*Cup launch.*] With Walt Whitman, I believe poetry—literature—can be "good health" to us, and "filter and fibre" our blood. [*Cup launch.*] I believe poetry is economic. [*Cup launch. Another cup launch. A third cup launch.*] I believe poetry is all about exchange and dialogue, and I think that the Internet is and will keep playing a central role for contemporary poetry, so as long as poets understand that the world is very diverse and complex and that the term "global" still has to find its true meaning, implying a respectful recognition of otherness, including that of other languages and cultures, because despite the bleakness and cruelty and sadism and perversity and violence and desperation and despondency and despair and hopelessness of human nature, I can't help feeling that there is still some hope left in this cold and bitter world!

[DAVID MOORHEAD *and* SHIRLEY WOOD *freeze.* BARISTA *turns fan off.* BARISTA *rolls a mop and bucket around the counter.*]

BARISTA [*Mopping as the light fades*]: God follows me around, mopping up my tears, but I say: "Let my tears stanch the earth's dry appetite, let my tears go forth into the heavens and be written before the face of the firmament, let my bow'd knees bend thy obdurate heart."

[*Curtain.*]

ANGRY AT GOD (A MYSTERY PLAY)

ANGRY AT GOD (A MYSTERY PLAY)

Performed at the Poetry Project, October 29, 2001. Directed by Drew Gardner, with the following cast:

BRITNEY	Katie Degentesh
SURFER	Drew Gardner
BARRY	Aaron Kieley
GOD	John Coletti

Scene One. *America.*

BRITNEY: Awww yeah "Only God knows why" right? right?? ... you masochistic sicko. You're my kind of opinion!

SURFER: Wearin' my lifeguard uniform shirt. Oh my God! Where did my long, beautiful hair go? New Structure sweater? Say cheese! I'm a leopard!

BARRY: ... groove ... for all the foxy people. Aww yeah. [*Music stops.*] The music???

BRITNEY [*as the first spasms hit her*]: Pop music sucks—though it taste like beer.

SURFER: Too bad you people don't make any goddamn sense.

BRITNEY: Look at the brand, hmmm?

BARRY: Awww yeah! Thats my kinda breakfast food!

BRITNEY: Makin' love, yeah!

BARRY: Awww yeah, baby ... Chester, get out of here, dude... we're bein' sexy—

SURFER: Now I'm nauseous ... god, now I'm nauseous ... I'm sorry, I feel bad ...

[*Curtain. End Scene One.*]

Scene Two.

BRITNEY: Uh, yeah, God? Yeah . . . OH! I gotta song request ...

GOD: ... you like them li'l crane? Awww yeah, you like your origami friend ... your creased edges. How's that? Yeah baby, that's right ...

BRITNEY [*Panting.*]: Oh Jesus, God … How do you … awww, yeah … how do you … awww God … do this … to me? …

GOD: … ROFLMAO!!! Megatron! your pad is full of red X's!!! AWWW YEAH!!!—Beer is proof that I love you and want you to be happy!

BRITNEY: … oh yeah … that's it … nice little kisses … awww yeah … Jesus … "thigh of a baby Jesus" … I'm coming!

GOD: Awww yeah … need I say more? check out the merchandise. And god said, Let there be Lips!

[*Curtain. End of Scene Two.*]

Scene Three.

SURFER: Jackass of a God, uhhh! Uhh, uhh! Unh! Uhh, unh, uhh! Unh …

BRITNEY: What the hell subculture of stupidity—

SURFER: Open your eyes, realize I'm BEIN' God—

GOD: … 01100100011101010110110101100010 …

BRITNEY: Some days I'm like God, and others? I am just plain better … awww yeah … my DVD movies … Hey God, remember when I said I love you? Forget it to hell! Heh heh whatever! [*Applies eyeliner.*] HOORAY for me!

SURFER: That shit fuckin' rocks!

[*Curtain. End of Scene Three.*]

Scene Four.

BARRY: I'm the water!

SURFER: I'm the dishes!

GOD: I'm the soap!

[*Curtain. End of Scene Four.*]

Scene Five.

BARRY: Oh my god, what a sight. SO SAD. Aww yeah. Aww yeah. Aww yeah. Aww yeah. Aww yeah. So beautiful, oh where am I? Aww yeah this is great ... Oh God let me live. Would I die for her? Death comes sooner or later. Mom ... Dad? Thank you ... saying awww but inside I'm thinking "God if chickens can dance better than her, how bad is she?"

BRITNEY: There's free chocolate? HAPPY!!! ... the chocolate's where it's AT.

BARRY: Oh god. I actually had fun tonight. I went out ... played this house condemned for Millie ... got the feeling from it ... mmm ... nonchalant? Believe so. Like, I saw you in the elevator today? You know ... you were so, like, "THAT never showed up on the CD."

BRITNEY: Is vibration brief description?

SURFER: It feels better if you say that god just called his number when you do we ... we keep it crackin like this ugh, aww yeah yeah yeah, it don't quit it ...

BARRY: So we spent our time with them...

BRITNEY: Aww yeah! Burning Man was insane, esp with the burning. Oh My Fucking God!! OMFG pretty much sums it up

BARRY: I want to ask you a bunch of questions and I ... [*Opens his arms waiting for the giant bosoms.*] ... OH MY GOD!!!! Come on my lovelies!! [BRITNEY *reaches into her shirt.*] AWW YEAH!!!! C'mon!!! OH MY GOD OH MY GOD, ITS LIKE STEVE JOBS JUST LOOKED AT SAUSAGEBOX.COM

BRITNEY: Yeah, I can tell, I'm the numbah ...

SURFER: Cheap shit, you wish! [*Sarcasm:*] In God we trust!

BRITNEY: Thank God it's Friday!

GOD: And speaking of God, how about this Jesus fella! I mean, who does He ... the chosen people know what I'm talkin' about. Aww yeah, anyone wants to call me please do so HAHA aww yeah I'm gonna be famous. Um you never see me anymore? You just see me *EVERY GOD DAMN DAY* ... I GUESS THAT ISN'T ENOUGH huh? Heh? The chosen people know what I'm talkin' about. Think you can compare with this? [Shakes it.] Aww yeah baby. LMAO!!! My ass IS God. Aww YEah!! I deserve your vote because ... because ... you guys are sick bastards. I am god. All girls want me. If you have to stoop to insulting me, it just shows your own insecurity. Aww yeah. Cheers. Thnak you. It creeps me ... to myself, like an illiterate miscreant, aww yeah! haha oh god. funny stuff. ... so cute and stuff ... shouldn't be this sick. Flowers, yeah ... love them. Love them with me. Share the love. Aww, yeah ... put your desk to be directly next to mine. Aww yeah. [*Runs over self.*]

BRITNEY: Oh my God!

BARRY: You kill yerself, buddy?

GOD: Yeah, I'm dead, man.

BARRY: Glad you made it, welcome to the farm.

GOD [*Snorts.*]: Aww yeah, Me Want: Tall Frozen Mocachino. [*To* BRITNEY.] Is that you playing air guitar on my soul?

BRITNEY: Like, LATE FOR CLASS!

GOD: Look at you jumping around like a friggin monkey. My god, I love you … so much. So much. [*Hands her a box filled with lingerie.*]

BRITNEY: You gave me clothes. I love you!

GOD: God, I'd love to place my hand—

BRITNEY: Four hands are better than two. SHIT! Oh god, you guys, I'm so close already ... ooh, shit yeah ... "hard candy" … Aww, shit, these fucking jeans ... have been a fleshy tiddy begging for ... yes, god! that is what it was! Movement! … aww yeah! …

GOD: Glad to hear it! That's just the way it is, aww yeah

BRITNEY: Oh god … Do it again ... [*Laughs.*] Woooo! God what are we ... Oh man we're going to a funktion

GOD: Yeah Yeah Yeah Aww Now come on and drop it for me ...

BRITNEY: Flame Resistant's Christ Core Crew Baby... Awwww yeah!

GOD: AWWWW HELL YEAH!!!!!!!!!!!!!!

BRITNEY: HEY GOD! Uh, yeah, God? Yeah . . . OH! I gotta nother song request!

GOD: GOT MY PIPE!!! AWWWW YEAH!!! GOD BLESS SOUNDWAVES!!!!!!!!!!!!!

[*Curtain.*]

BARKING SPIDERS
BEARDED CLAMS
BANANA HAMMOCKS
B.O. EXPRESS
BALL MOVEMENTS
BELCH'N BUZZARDS
BEN DOVER ALL STARS
B-B-B
BUH
BITTER MIDGETS
BUH
BUH BUH BOOB WATCHERS
BUD-WEISER STATE UNIVER-SITY
B-B-B-
BUMPING MONKEYS
BRECKENRIDGE BARKING SNOW SPIDERS
BEER CLUB FOR MEN
BUH BUH BUH
BANG BANG MACHINE
BUH BUH BUH
BANG BANG MACHINE B-B-
BUH BUH
B-B-B-BIDDLE BADDLE
BUH BUH BUH

"B": A ROAD MOVIE

"B": A ROAD MOVIE

LEONARD
BARBARA
DUTCH
RADIO
RITA
CHORUS OF AUTOMOBILES
STATE TROOPER

Scene One: *They are driving aimlessly. America.*

LEONARD: Barking Spiders, Bearded Clams, Banana Hammocks, Beer Club for Men, Ball Movements … What's the difference between a blonde and a bowling ball?

BARBARA: You don't eat your bowling ball.

DUTCH: Mmmm … creamy … thick … I get the munchies bowling and dancing to live
sauce …

BARBARA: Blondes are virtually in the dark without fluorescent bowling balls.

DUTCH: Between the dark and the thyme soufflé ... mmmm …

LEONARD: B.O. Express, Belch'n Buzzards, Belly Poppin' Fat Boys, Ben Dover All Stars, Bitter Midgets …

BARBARA [*Yawns*]: Breathable air is totally overrated. Salmon the size of bowling balls …

DUTCH [*Picking up on her reverie*]: Lobster fingerling potato salad meticulously arranged, gypsy-style, with gulf shrimp or scallions …

BARBARA [*In a state of REM*]: New Maximum Capacity Beancurd stuffed with shrimp paste in soya sauce ...

LEONARD: Boob Watchers, Breckenridge Barking Snow Spiders, Budweiser State University, Bumping Monkeys—

BARBARA [*Arms flailing*]: Barbara's Bowling Luncheon Cake!

LEONARD: Brew City Pop Tops, Big Dog Gotta Eat, Boy Chunders, Bums with Nice Luggage … What's the difference between a blonde and a bowling ball wearing pantyhose? [*He turns on the radio, channel surfs.*]

BARBARA [*Waking, sleepily*]: ... something about the "balance hole"?

RADIO: The tape, which was discovered about 10 days ago in an abandoned apartment in Jalalabad, Afghanistan, was described to reporters by the—

LEONARD [*Snapping the radio off*]: You know, I can't imagine somebody like bin Laden understanding the joy of Hanukkah, or the joy of Christmas, celebrating peace and hope. This man wants to destroy any semblance of civilization for his own power and his own good. [*As he burps*]: After some beer, the blonde has to press the tilde (~) to pee ...

BARBARA: Fact!

DUTCH: I don't get it.

[*Curtain. End of Scene One.*]

Scene Two: *Fast food drive-thru.*

RITA [*From speaker*]: I am Living Water, a submissive woman. Order on-line ... release your pain ... I am the message that Christ's come again.

LEONARD [*Loudly, leaning out car window, into intercom mic*]: Uhhh, can I get two double-decker supremes, a chicken chalupa-wrap, a, uh nacho cheeseburger, uh, the uh, and, uh—what do you guys want to drink?

RITA [*Speaker noise*]: I am the water that quenches your thirst, I am the last, I was the first. I am one with what the tree vole drinks.

BABARA [*Yelling over* LEONARD*'s shoulder*]: Hey, why does Jesus never say, "I am the water of life"?

DUTCH: That's a very good question.

RITA [*More speaker noise*]: I am the elf in the trees. I am the mermaid of your peach. I am the water's wash of flame's desire. See my quest in the words you hear, in the songs of the no-wind-in-there.

LEONARD [*Snorts*]: ... I am Big Water, Big Water is me!

RITA [*Encouraged*]: I am the ocean, the lake, the river, pond and creek. I am the
mountains, the valleys, the desert and the trees. I am Earth ...

DUTCH: ... *Ich bin der Dreck unter deinen Walzen, Ich bin dein geheimer Schmutz Und verlorenes Metallgeld, Ich bin deine Ritze, Ich bin ...*

BARBARA: God, I feel like I'm drinking water ...

RITA: Air I am. Fire I am. Water, earth and Spirit I am. Breeze I am. Sun I am. Brook, Mountain and Goddess ...

CHORUS OF AUTOMOBILES: Honk! Honk! HONK!

BARBARA: I'm wearing: Hot Pink & Black Zebra Striped Skirt, Black Lace Trimmed Shirt. Soon I will have vegetarian un-chicken nuggets with everything that lives in water. Until then, I'm gnawing on water—

LEONARD [*Forcefully, into intercom mic*]: You are my licorice. I am your dandelion; you are my first wish. I am your water wings; you are my deep. I am your open arms; you are my running leap.

BARBARA and DUTCH: I am the house that protects you I am the car that takes you places I am the water that you drink I am the food that you eat I am the pencil that you write—

RITA [*Speaker noise*]: My name is Orianna. I am a rainbow goddess. I am water, gas and sunshine. I live in the clouds. I make rainbows. I feel happy because I'm making other kids ... oh, wait, no [*Sudden shame.*] ... pride ... ohhh ... pride ... my ... scalp ... begins to tighten. Have mercy! Lord, I am afraid! Water, I thirst, I thirst!

LEONARD [*Shouting into intercom mic*]: I am like water, whose surface you have disturbed! You see your reflection in me - distorted!

RITA [*Sudden strength*]: I AM THE THUNDERBOLT AMONG WEAPONS, AND I AM THE WATER GOD AND THE NAMES. I AM THE CONTROLLER OF DEATH.

[*Curtain. End of Scene Two.*]

Scene Three: *A mountain overpass.*

LEONARD: So he was Arabic looking and my mother said something like "Oh my god. Look out he is Arabic." and I almost jumped out of the car.

DUTCH [*Shivers*]: Things scare me.

BARBARA: OH MY GOD! LOOK OUT BEHIND YOU! Haha. Made you look. Oh. You didn't look?

LEONARD: I can't! My bangs are choking me!!

DUTCH: Oh my God, look out! There's a lizard or something in the middle of the street!

LEONARD [*Flips on the radio in his panic*]: I can't see!!!

RADIO: OH MY GOD!! LOOK OUT BEHIND YOU!!!!!

[Curtain. End of Scene Three.]

Scene Four: *Night. They huddle in the car parked on the side of the road.*

BARBARA: Crickets and grasshoppers ...

DUTCH: ... the sounds of crickets courting ... a rice weevil larva eating inside a wheat kernel ...

LEONARD: Birds, amphibians, reptiles, and mammals ...

DUTCH: ... waves at the beach, with katydids and crickets chirping, waterfalls, fountains, waves, crickets, and katydids ...

BARBARA: Shhhh ... birds, mammals, frogs ... oh! Big cat growl!

DUTCH: Birds ... chicken? Crickets, crow, cow-moo ...

LEONARD: Ah! Ah! Listen! Tinkling ground crickets prefer oak-leaf litter for their sweet, ringing sounds ...

BARBARA: Crickets, crickets: "Cript closed crowd at hockey"—

DUTCH [*Yawns*]: Creaks and groans—ghostly sounds ...

LEONARD: The shrill call of a big, green cicada ...

BARBARA: Ghost crabs, scale worms, what sounds like large springs boinging ...

DUTCH: Big black furry space ...

LEONARD [*Drifting off*]: Killer wasps vacating their purchase as bigfoot approaches ...

DUTCH: Sounds like a completely ghost-inhabited castle ...

LEONARD: Steady beat of some grease ants ... the antennae of white-winged ghost moths receiving sound ...

BARBARA [*Curled up, sighs*]: ... husk of a cicada's chirp stone silent seed pods split a crackle of ... moonrise sounds ... I hear a dark river fill a curved path ...

LEONARD [*Nearly asleep*]: Shhh, listen: Bird nests, cicada shells, honey combs, pine cones ...

DUTCH: Little scissors?

LEONARD [*Yawns*]: Bug legs. Berry peckers ... like, "dug-g-dug-g" ...

BARBARA [*Drifting off*]: A transparent sound, ghost-like, hanging in the air ... between oaks and willows ...

[Curtain. End of Scene Four.]

Scene Five: *Morning. On the road again.*

DUTCH: Ahhhhh, the smell of sun-drenched morning coffee!

BARBARA: But with this diuretic, you feel it: The price.

LEONARD: Fluid coffee causes much excitement in the brain ... like a shot of the RISING SUN. Sayyyy, anyone care to infuse a little sexuality into the—

STATE TROOPER: Beee-ooop!

[*They pull over.*]

LEONARD: Boy—well, color me happy, Officer—am I glad to see you! Listen: I need your stories and input. All cops have stories. I'm looking for stories about your first pursuit. [*Rummages around.*] Complimentary morning coffee? Newspaper?

STATE TROOPER: Bah! I'm sick of people who "do the police" in different voices. [*Slaps* LEONARD.] Here's what I want you to do. Just get on up and dance. Wave your hands from side to side. Just get on up out your seat and move ...

BARBARA: Wow! What's your phone number?

STATE TROOPER [*Pulls* LEONARD *from the car.*] Now I feel lots better! IT'S FRIIIDAAAAY!! Aww yeah, baby! Life is good: people are crazy! [*Repeatedly slaps* LEONARD.]

LEONARD: Ow! Ow! Imagining what is suppose to be a really

cool place ... "generous bedrooms, deep tubs with separate shower cubicles ..."

BARBARA [*Getting out of car to flirt*]: BTW, my actual name is: "wouldn't U like 2 know" ... *wink wink*

LEONARD: ... Bed, Bath & Beyond ... Sam's Club ...

STATE TROOPER: What are you going to do about it! I'm peein' on ya and you're just sitting there and takin' it! You wanna know why? Because I—

LEONARD: Jumpin' Bean ... Bazaar del Mundo ... Bird N' Berry Creations ... Boutiqueri ...

DUTCH [*Suddenly aware of the commotion*]: O clement, o loving, o sweet Virgin Mary, pray for us, O holy Mother of God!

BARBARA [*Disturbed now*]: Brrrr. I want to go. The light is bright, yellow and round. The highway is filling up. Is this is my final destination? I thought it was Newark.

DUTCH [*Weeping*]: I just want to find the right therapist.

STATE TROOPER [*Turns to* DUTCH *and* BARBARA]: BY THE WAY, I'VE BEEN ON TESTOSTERONE FOR THREE YEARS, LIVING MY LIFE LEGALLY, THANK YOU. Before that I was at the nadir, I was like the railway passed through a crumbling archway here, and filling the valley ahead, my final destination.

LEONARD: ... Barnes & Noble ... Burger King ... Borders ... Big Boy ...

STATE TROOPER: DON'T BLAME ME.

DUTCH: But, no, uh [*coughs*] ...

BARBARA: ... beyond blame.

DUTCH: Blame it on Nader.

BARBARA: I blame Internet chat rooms.

LEONARD: ... obnoxious music in the background ...

BARBARA: Blame Clinton.

DUTCH: Blame Bush.

BARBARA: Romeo and Juliet—who was to blame?

LEONARD: ... Bally Gaming ...

STATE TROOPER: Blame history
DUTCH: Belly-dancing

BARBARA: Israel apportions blame Palestinian demonstrators in the thick of battle

LEONARD: ... Banana Republic ...

DUTCH: *Whoa-oah Black Betty, blam-a-lam*

LEONARD: ... Blockbuster ... B. Dalton ...

STATE TROOPER: Blame bohemianism

LEONARD: ... Baskin Robbins ...

BARBARA: Das Ballycotton Ballyhoo Ballyhoo Ballyhoo Bask Bask bassART Bates ...

DUTCH: Bomb Circle Bomb Circle Bond, Tony feat ... Sabine Brüder, Die Bug Burger

LEONARD: Bombo ... Burger Chase, Burger Time Burger ...

BARBARA: ... Balloon Raid, bamboo, bananas ... bogart ... bomb threat

STATE TROOPER: Bomb Squad, the Ballistix Balloon Raid

Ballyhoo Ballz Banana Drama Bandana

DUTCH: Balls of Steel. Bureaucracy Time ...

LEONARD: Bolt, bomb, bonk, boot, bop, bounce, bout, box

BARBARA: Brew, broil, bug, burn, bust, butt

STATE TROOPER: Bad, bah, bam, bang, bash, blah

DUTCH: BAD MOON RISING BAD SEED BADESALZ BAEZ ... BANG BANG MACHINE BANG BANG MACHINE BANKS, BE BOP DELUXE, BURN BURN BURN

LEONARD: Bad old days; Bad to me; Badge; Bahama; Blue jean bop; Blue magic; Blue Boom bang a bang; Boom boom; Boom ...

BARBARA: BOOTYLICIOUS!

STATE TROOPER: Be-Bop-a-Lu-La!

DUTCH: Bang-a Boomerang bang-a boomerang!

LEONARD: B-b-bu biddle baddle ...

BARBARA: blllhhhuhhh ... bllllhuuhhhh ...

DUTCH: Buh ... uhhhhh ... buh.

LEONARD: Buh!

STATE TROOPER: Buh.

DUTCH and BARBARA: Buh!

STATE TROOPER, BARBARA and LEONARD: Buh!

DUTCH: Buh!

LEONARD: Buh!

BARBARA and LEONARD: Buh!

ALL: Buh!

DUTCH: Buh!

ALL:
Buh! Buh!

[*Curtain.*]

ABOUT THE WORK

These pieces were all written for, and first posted to, the Flarflist, an e-mail listserv founded in 2001. Dialog was mostly written by using the results of a variety of different Internet searches, often around similar themes or kinds of phrases.

"Mozart & Salieri" is a Google translation of Pushkin's play of the same title. I ran searches on each line of an English-language translation of the play, and rewrote—or "translated"—it, picking and choosing from the results.

"The Separation of Church and State" and "Written in Styrofoam" were written within days of each other in 2007, the latter largely from posts to the SUNY Buffalo Poetics Listserv and various blogs maintained by poets and others.

"Lysistrata" was written for a publication party for the magazine *Pompom*. The goal was to use something from each contributor in each issue to date of the magazine. The goal, sadly, was impossible, and only one contribution to the magazine survives in the final version of the play: Rob Fitterman's "This Window Makes Me Feel."

I never imagined these things performed—they were meant to be read on the page (or screen)—but by some miracle, some of them made their way to the stage. My thanks to everyone involved the various productions.

Gary Sullivan is the author of *Dead Man*, *How to Proceed in the Arts*, *Swoon* (with Nada Gordon), and three issues of a comic book, *Elsewhere*. His poetry, criticism, and comics have appeared in numerous journals, weeklies, and anthologies, including *The Consequence of Innovation: 21st Century Poetics*, *LA Weekly*, *Multicultural Review*, *Nineteen Lines: A Drawing Center Writing Anthology*, *Rain Taxi*, *SF Weekly*, and *The Gertrude Stein Awards in Innovative American Poetry*. His plays have been performed in San Francisco and New York City, at Intersection for the Arts, the Lab, the Marsh, Medicine Show, and other venues. In early 2001 he co-founded the Flarflist Collective with half a dozen other poets and guest-edited an issue of *Chain* focused on comics. In 2002-03 he co-edited the *Poetry Project Newsletter* with Nada Gordon. He lives in Brooklyn, New York, with Nada and their two cats, Dante and Nemo.

ROOF BOOKS

the best in language since 1976

Recent Titles

- Dworkin, Craig, editor. **The Consequence of Innovation: 21st Century Poetics.** 304p. $29.95
- Nasdor, Marc. **Sonnetailia.** 80p. $12.95
- Gordon, Nada. **Folly.** 128p. $13.95
- Shaw, Lytle, editor. **Nineteen Lines: A Drawing Center Writing Anthology.** 336p. $24.95
- Arakawa, Gins, Madeline. **Making Dying Illegal.** 224p. $22.95.
- Stefans, Brian Kim. **Kluge.** 128p. $13.95
- Perelman, Bob. **Iflife.** 140p. $13.95.
- Guest, Barbara. **Dürer in the Window, Reflexions on Art.** Book design by Richard Tuttle. Four color throughout. 80p. $24.95.

ROOF BOOKS are published by
Segue Foundation • 300 Bowery • New York, NY 10012
Visit our website at **seguefoundation.com**
for a complete list of books

ROOF BOOKS are distributed by
SMALL PRESS DISTRIBUTION
1341 Seventh Avenue • Berkeley, CA. 94710-1403.
Phone orders: 800-869-7553
spdbooks.org